Carefree Clothes for Girls

Carefree Clothes for Girls

20 Patterns for Outdoor Frocks, Playdate Dresses, and More

Junko Okawa

TRUMPETER
Boston & London
2009

Contents

Introduction
Thinking of a Smiling Little Girl as I Draw

COTTON AND LINEN, rinsed and then dried in the sun, several layers of gauze, unhemmed edges, hand stitching, antique lace trim—girls' clothes with a distinctive mood.

As my hands move, ideas come forth. I'll add a stitch here and this button there, and that lace I set aside seems just right for making it perfectly cute. Creative ideas from the heart are essential for these clothes. That's why these handmade outfits are unique.

Even if you're not skilled at sewing, clothes that are made with love are imbued with a feeling that can't be bought at any price. Making clothes like this brings me joy. I hope that each little girl who wears these clothes feels happy and content.

As I designed these clothes, I imagined a very lively little girl who has an uncanny ability to cheer up everyone around her. I call this collection of designs Uonca, which is my phonetic spelling of the Polish word for "meadow." While meadows often don't attract much attention, they are a vibrant and essential part of the landscape. I hope that the girls who wear these clothes will feel as essential and vibrant as a lovely green meadow.

Spring & Summer

Apron and Pants

The apron is made of sturdy sailcloth, with a flower-print pocket made of cotton that has been washed for softness and leather trim as fine as a pen drawing. The apron is paired with lace-trimmed pants.

Instructions for the apron on page 45.
Instructions for the pants on page 47.

Babushka-Style Scarf

Recalling the scarves worn by Russian grandmothers, this babushka scarf is made of fringed cotton in a small flower print and trimmed with fine lace. Take all these features favored by little girls and sew them together with tiny stitches.

Instructions on page 44.

Blouse with Crocheted Doily Trim

The unfinished hem contrasts the fine lace trim, which is made by taking a square doily and cutting it to fit the edge of the collar. Finish it with gold-colored stitches.

❦❦❦ ❦❦❦ ❦❦❦ ❦❦❦

Instructions on page 49.

Natural Cotton Skirt

This skirt has a thick waistband that forms a yoke, layers of three types of unprocessed cotton, and an unfinished hem. The ruffle on the left side of the hem adds a touch of charm.

❦❦❦ ❦❦❦ ❦❦❦ ❦❦❦

Instructions on page 52.

Bag

The thick, unhemmed handle and the slightly off-kilter style of this bag will look great on anyone. A fancy lace doily is set into a sturdy base of rough cotton.

Instructions on page 56.

Dress with Lace Doily

This white cotton dress has an antique doily sewn on to look like a pocket. Use the edge of the doily that is cut off as trim for the collar.

❧❧❧ ❧❧❧ ❧❧❧ ❧❧❧

Instructions on page 60.

White Cotton and Flower Print Sundress

The high-waisted bodice is in a rose-bud print. The pocket is made of a random patchwork of floral prints.

❧❧ ❧❧ ❧❧ ❧❧

Instructions on page 63.

Chemise

An adorable gauze chemise mimics those used for underwear in France in former days. This simple shape, which can be adapted into either a blouse or a dress, is decorated with delicate lace and silver stitching.

Instructions on page 66.

Black Linen Hat

This hat, made of layers of fabric stitched together, is adorned with random pieces of lace. Slightly oversized, it lies low on the head.

❧❧❧ ❧❧❧ ❧❧❧ ❧❧❧

Instructions on page 58.

Dress with Quilted Bodice

This dress is made of soft, double gauze fabric. The quilted bodice has a cotton backing, and the skirt is lined with gauze of a contrasting texture.

✧✧✧ ✧✧✧ ✧✧✧ ✧✧✧

Instructions on page 69.

Crossover Tunic

This plain linen tunic is given a folk-loric touch with lace. Much of its charm lies in its ability to be worn with a wide variety of garments, such as a camisole or a heavy shirt.

❧❧❧ ❧❧❧ ❧❧❧ ❧❧❧

Instructions on page 73.

Dress with Ruffle Trim

Easy to throw on at the last minute, this dress has ruffles that create a capped sleeve effect. The hem is left unfinished, and with repeated washing, it takes on an appealingly worn look.

❦❦❦ ❦❦❦ ❦❦❦ ❦❦❦

Instructions on page 76.

Autumn & Winter

White Melton Hat and Pants

The front of this hat is folded back to make a brim. The black color of the hand stitching and the buttons set off the wearer's rosy cheeks. Lace-trimmed pants and a striped shirt complete the outfit.

❧❧ ❧❧ ❧❧ ❧❧

Instructions for the hat on page 90.
Instructions for the pants on page 95.

Pants with Leg Warmers

Made of the same material as sweat-pants, these pants feature a patch that looks like an afterthought, giving the outfit a whimsical air. Knitted leg warmers are sewn onto the pants to make them warm and cozy for chilly days.

◦◦◦◦ ◦◦◦◦ ◦◦◦◦ ◦◦◦◦

Instructions on page 79.

Scarf

This patchwork scarf is made of remnants from the other fabrics used in this book. Add antique lace, hand stitching, buttons, maybe even bells, to give it a unique handmade look.

❧❧❧ ❧❧❧ ❧❧❧ ❧❧❧

Instructions on page 88.

Dress with Contrasting Patches

This "Cinderella" dress has contrasting patches sewn on almost as an afterthought.
Buttons of varied colors and shapes line the sides of the back opening.

※ ※ ※ ※

Instructions on page 82.

Lace-Trimmed Coat

This natural linen coat is lined with unbleached cotton. Buttons of slightly varying colors, hand stitching, and elegant lace give it an antique look.

✦✧✦ ✦✧✦ ✦✧✦ ✦✧✦

Instructions on page 85.

Coat with Scarf

This black Melton cloth coat looks almost like a blazer. The finely knit scarf is sewn to the back of the collar, and the coat itself is cut short for ease of movement.

❧❧ ❧❧ ❧❧ ❧❧

Instructions on page 92.

How to Make It!

Things to Remember When Using Patterns and Making Clothes

This book comes with actual-size patterns for the clothes and hats pictured here.

You can make all the clothes and hats in this book using the enclosed actual-size patterns. However, there are no patterns for the babushka scarf, the bag, or the scarves. Make these three items without using a pattern by trimming and sewing the fabric into triangles or squares. Patterns are also available as individual PDFs for download at www.makegoodbooks.com.

The clothes come in four sizes and the hats in three.

The patterns for the clothes come in four sizes for girls: 4, 5, 6, and 7. The patterns for the hats come in small, medium, and large.

Before sewing, decide which size you need using the measurements on the sizing chart on the next page. The sizes given are approximations of standard U.S. sizes. The best way to determine your child's size is to measure him or her. If your child is between sizes, refer to the instruction pages to find the item's finished size and adjust the pattern as necessary.

Copy the patterns onto a separate sheet of paper.

The instructions tell you which actual-size pattern to use, so identify the pattern you need and trace the lines that indicate the proper size onto a separate sheet of paper. Trace along the lines carefully with a marker or other instrument.

You should trace the lines that indicate openings and gathers as well as the ones that indicate the outlines of the garment.

Some parts of the items, especially simple things, such as straight skirts or pockets, are not included in the actual-size patterns. Make your own patterns for these components using the measurements on the instructions page.

Write in the positions of the buttons and pockets yourself.

In order to keep the patterns from becoming too complicated, some patterns leave out indications of where the buttons and pockets go. In those cases, the measurements are shown on the instructions page, so draw them in yourself.

Add your own seam allowance to the fabric before cutting it.

These patterns do not include seam allowances. The necessary seam allowance is indicated in the diagrams on the instructions pages, so use the measurements there as your guide. After tracing a pattern to a separate sheet of paper, measure and draw the seam allowance around the pattern before cutting it out.

Attach decorations and lace carefully, with an eye toward balance of the elements.

You can decorate the garment with lace or ruffles, or make patchwork with remnants or doilies. The most balanced and appropriate position and size for these decorations will differ depending on the shape and texture of the doily or what kind of lace you use. It will be difficult for you to obtain the same lace or doilies, so I haven't indicated the exact positions or measurements. Refer to the photos in the front of the book or the drawings of finished garments to figure out what amounts of decorations and what positions will create the best balance.

Finish the garment by washing it.

After you finish sewing these garments, you should launder them to bring out their texture. This is true not only for cotton and linen but also for wool. Laundering will allow the thread ends of unhemmed garments to become part of the design.

Sizes

Size: 4, 5, 6, 7
Chest: 21¼", 22⅞", 24½", 26"
Waist: 19¾", 20½", 21¾", 22½"
Hip: 22½", 24", 25⅝", 26⅞"
Height: 39⅜", 43¼", 47¼", 51¼"

Sizes for Hats

Size: Small, Medium, Large
Head circumference: 20½", 21¾", 22½"

Babushka-Style Scarf

Photograph on page 11.

Finished Measurements

For sizes 4 and 5: about 15" × 15"
For sizes 6 and 7: about 15¾" × 15¾"

Materials

* Pattern: No pattern necessary
* Fabric: Flower print cotton,
  17¾" × 17 ¾"
* Lace A: 15¾" × ¾"
* Lace B: 23⅝" × ⅜"
* Lace C: 27½" of scalloped lace
* Embroidery floss: Gold, as needed

Instructions

1. **Cut the fabric.** Cut the fabric into a triangle following the measurements in Figure 1.
2. **Make fringe.** Pull out ⅜" to ⅝" of threads on two sides to form fringe. *See Figure 2.*
3. **Hem the edge.** Zigzag stitch along the long edge of the triangle; fold the edge under once toward the wrong side and machine stitch. *See Figure 3.*
4. **Finish the scarf.** Machine stitch each strip of lace onto the scarf as shown in Figure 4. Trim the scalloped detail off of the scalloped lace and use it as a tie for the scarf. Using one strand of the gold embroidery floss, hand stitch a simple running stitch along the fringed edges. *See Figure 4.*

Figure 1

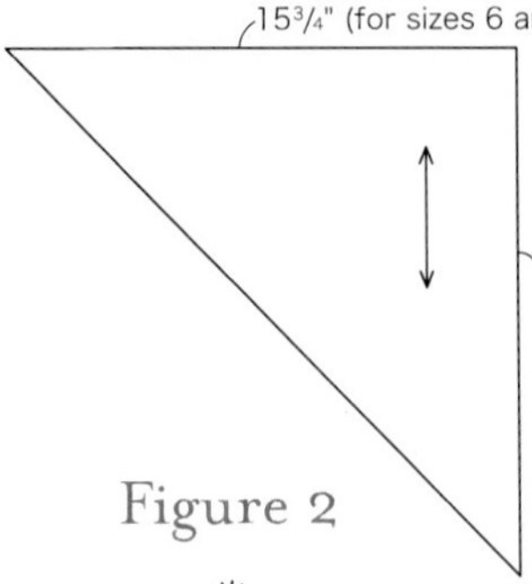

15" (for sizes 4 and 5)
15¾" (for sizes 6 and 7)

15"
15¾"

Figure 2

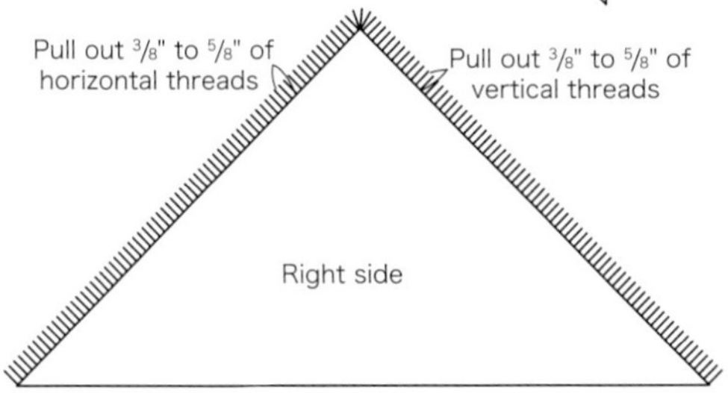

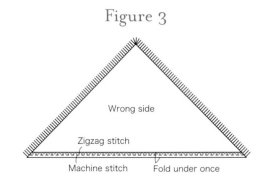

Pull out ⅜" to ⅝" of horizontal threads

Pull out ⅜" to ⅝" of vertical threads

Right side

Figure 3

Wrong side

Zigzag stitch

Machine stitch   Fold under once

Figure 4

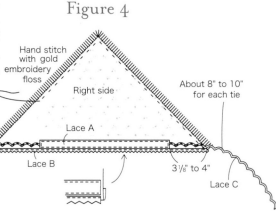

Hand stitch with gold embroidery floss

Right side

About 8" to 10" for each tie

Lace A

Lace B

3⅛" to 4"

Lace C

Apron

Photograph on page 10.

Finished Measurements (for sizes 4, 5, 6, and 7, respectively)

Chest: 25¼", 26¾", 28 ⅜", 29⅞"
Garment length: 15⅛", 16⅜", 17½", 18 ¾"

Materials

* Pattern: 1-B from pattern insert (2 pattern pieces)
* Fabric: Sail cloth, 59⅛" wide. For sizes 4 and 5: 19¾"; for sizes 6 and 7:23⅝"
* Contrasting fabric: Flower print cotton, 15¾" × 9⅞"
* Button: 1, ⅞" in diameter
* Cap rivets: 4 pairs, ¼" in diameter
* Leather strip: 1¼" × ⅜"
* Lace thread, as needed

Instructions

1. **Cut out the pattern pieces.** Following the shorter version of pattern 1-B in the back of the book, and referring to Figure 1, trace the patterns for the bodice front and bodice back onto a separate sheet of paper.

2. **Cut the fabric.** Fold your fabric in half, selvage to selvage, right sides together, and position the pattern pieces as shown in Figure 2. Add seam allowances to the pieces as shown before cutting them out. Cut the fabric for the pocket (following the measurements in Figure 1) from the contrasting fabric.

3. **Attach the pocket.** First fold the pocket opening under twice toward

the wrong side, and machine stitch twice, creating two rows. Crease the seam allowance on the other three sides with an iron. Hand stitch the side hems with lace thread about ¼" in from the outside edge. Position the pocket on the bodice front, and machine stitch it in place along three sides. Hand stitch down the center of the pocket to divide the pocket in two.

4. **Hem the back.** On the two bodice back pieces, fold the seam allowance of the back opening under toward the wrong side. Machine stitch it in place twice.

5. **Attach the bodice front and back.** Place the bodice front and back pieces right sides together, and sew the pieces together along the shoulders and the sides. Press the seam allowances open.

6. **Finish the seams.** Zigzag along the bottom edge of the apron to prevent fraying. Fold the seam allowance for the bottom hem under, and machine stitch it in place twice. Fold the seam allowance under for each armhole, and stitch it in place. Fold the seam allowance under for the neckline, and stitch in place twice. Using a running stitch, hand stitch along the neckline with lace thread.

7. **Finish the apron.** Position the leather strip on the left chest area in a well-balanced position and hand sew it in place. Then insert the rivets at the four corners of the pockets.

8. **Add a buttonhole and button.** Make a buttonhole at the back neckline, and sew a button on the opposite side.

Figure 1

Pattern Details for I-B

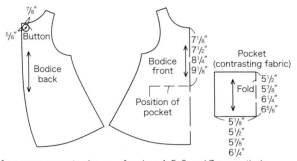

The four measurements given are for sizes 4, 5, 6, and 7, respectively

Figure 2

Apron Layout

The seam allowance is ⅜" unless otherwise indicated

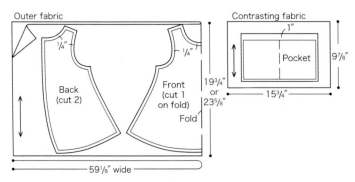

Figure 3

Finished Apron

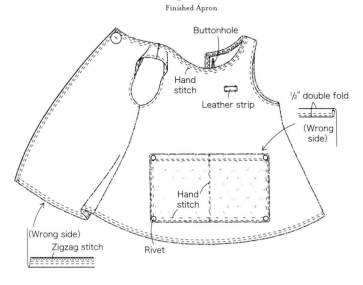

Pants

Photograph on page 10.

Finished Measurements (for sizes 4, 5, 6, and 7, respectively)

Hips: 29⅛", 30¾", 32¼", 33⅞"
Length (waist to ankle): 18⅛", 20", 21⅝", 23¼"

Materials

* Pattern: 2-I from pattern insert (1 pattern piece)
* Fabric: Lightweight cotton, 43⅜" wide. For sizes 4 and 5: 23⅝"; for size 6 and 7: 39⅜"
* Lace: 2¾" wide. For sizes 4 and 5: 35 ½"; for sizes 6 and 7: 39⅜"
* Elastic tape: ¼" wide and slightly shorter than the waist measurement

Instructions

1. **Cut out the pattern piece.** Following pattern 2-I in the back of the book, and referring to Figure I, trace the pattern for the pants onto a separate sheet of paper.
2. **Cut the fabric.** Fold the fabric in half, right sides together, and position the pattern piece as shown in Figure 2. Add seam allowances to the fabric as shown before cutting it.
3. **Sew the inner leg seams.** Fold the pants left in half, right sides together. Sew along the inner leg seam, and finish the seam allowance with zigzag stitches. Repeat for the pants right.
4. **Make the lace trim.** Cut two pieces of lace to the length of the circumference of the leg openings, plus ¾". Sew the two ends of the lace together to form a circle, leaving a ⅜" seam allowance.
5. **Attach the lace.** Turn the pants right side out, and place the lace rings over the bottom of the pants, right sides together. Stitch the lace in place, and finish the seam allowances with zigzag stitches. Turn the lace right side out, fold the seam allowance under toward the wrong side, and press. *See Figure 3.*
6. **Sew pants left and right together.** Place the pants left on the pants right, right sides together, aligning the top edge and inner leg seams. Sew along the front, crotch, and back seams, and finish the seam allowances with zigzag stitches. Cut some stitches along the front seam within the seam allowance at the top edge for passing the elastic through.
7. **Finish the pants top.** Fold the top seam allowance under twice, and sew it in place. Pass the elastic through the gap created in the previous step. Stitch the ends of the elastic together, and then hand stitch the gap closed. *See Figure 3.*

Figure 1

Pattern Details for 2-1

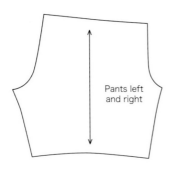

Pants left and right

Figure 2

Pants Layout

Seam allowances are 3/8" unless otherwise indicated.

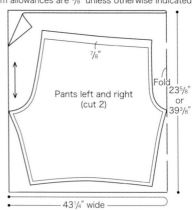

7/8"

Pants left and right
(cut 2)

Fold

23 5/8"
or
39 3/8"

43 1/4" wide

Figure 3

Finished Pants

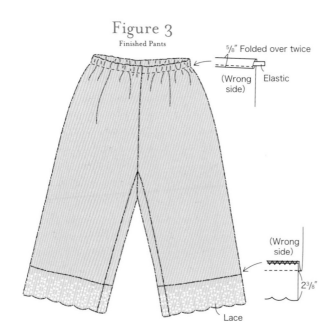

5/8" Folded over twice

(Wrong side)

Elastic

(Wrong side)

2 3/8"

Lace

Blouse with Crocheted Doily Trim

Photograph on page 12.

Finished Measurements (for sizes 4, 5, 6, and 7, respectively)

Chest: 25¼", 26¾", 28⅜", 30"
Length: 15⅛", 16⅜", 17½", 18¼"

Materials

* Pattern: 1-B from pattern insert (3 pattern pieces)
* Fabric: Indian cotton, 27½" wide. For sizes 4 and 5: 39⅜"; for sizes 6 and 7: 47¼"
* One lace doily
* Button: 1, ⅜" in diameter
* Embroidery floss: Gold, as needed

Instructions

1. **Cut out the pattern pieces.** Following the shorter version of pattern 1-B in the back of the book, and referring to Figure 1, trace the patterns for the bodice front, bodice back, and the sleeve onto a separate sheet of paper.
2. **Cut the fabric pieces.** Position the pattern pieces on the fabric as shown in Figure 2. Add seam allowances to the fabric as shown before cutting it. Cut the fabric for the bias binding on a 45° angle to the fabric grain to the exact measurements indicated.
3. **Finish the fabric edges.** Using a zigzag stitch, sew along the sides and shoulders of the bodice front and the two back pieces to keep the fabric from fraying, making sure the zigzag stitch stays within the seam allowance. Do not zigzag around the bottom edge.
4. **Sew the blouse back.** Place the two

pieces for the blouse back right sides together. Sew the pieces together from the bottom of the back opening down to the hem. Press the seam allowance open, and stitch around the back opening. *See Figure 3.*

5. **Attach the doily.** Cut the doily to fit the front neckline. Lay it on the right side of the front bodice, and sew it in place close to the edge along the neckline and the shoulder seams. *See Figure 4.*
6. **Sew the front and back together.** Place the bodice front on the bodice back, right sides together. Sew along the shoulders and press the seam allowance open. Do not sew the side seams at this point.
7. **Attach the binding to the neckline.** Lay the blouse flat, right side up. Place the wider binding for the neckline on the blouse, aligning the edges. Sew the binding in place close to the edge. Fold the binding under, toward the wrong side, and press. Fold the raw edge of the binding under, toward the wrong side, and press. Machine stitch in place, tucking the ends of the binding under at the back opening. Using one strand of the gold embroidery floss, create decorative hand stitches around the neckline. *See Figure 5.*
8. **Sew the side seams.** Place the blouse front and back with right sides together. Sew along both side seams, and press the seam allowance open.
9. **Prevent fraying.** Sew along the bottom edge of the blouse twice to prevent fraying.
10. **Attach the binding to the armholes.** Finish the shoulder openings by sewing the binding around them. Using the narrower binding for the armholes,

place the binding around the armholes, right sides together. Sew and finish as for the neckline binding (see step 7).

11. **Make the sleeves.** Edge stitch around the sleeve fabric to prevent fraying. Baste along the outside edge of the sleeve twice. Pull the ends of the thread to gather the fabric to make ruffles. Place the wrong side of each ruffle along the top of the right side of the armhole. Make sure each ruffle is centered over the shoulder and sew them in place. *See Figure 6.*

12. **Finish the blouse.** Make a thread loop following the instructions on page 68. Attach the loop to the back opening and sew the button on the opposite side. *See Figure 7.*

Figure 1

Pattern Details for 1-B

Sleeve

Bodice back

Bodice back

Figure 2

Blouse Layout

Seam allowances are ³/₈" unless otherwise indicated.

Back (cut 1)

Back (cut 1)

Binding for armholes

Binding for neckline

⁷/₈"

39³/₈" or 47¹/₄"

Sleeve (cut 1)

1¹/₈"

Sleeve (cut 1)

Front (cut 1)

—27¹/₂" wide—

Length of binding fabric (for sizes 4, 5, 6, and 7, respectively)

Size	4	5	6	7
For neckline	19³/₄"	19³/₄"	21⁵/₈"	21⁵/₈"
For sleeve opening	15³/₄"	15³/₄"	17³/₄"	17³/₄"

Figure 3

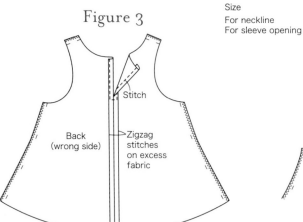

Stitch

Back (wrong side)

Zigzag stitches on excess fabric

Figure 4

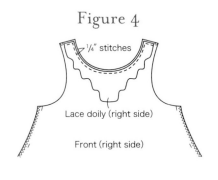

¹/₄" stitches

Lace doily (right side)

Front (right side)

Figure 5

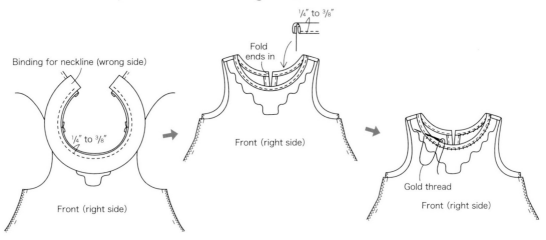

Binding for neckline (wrong side)

¼" to ⅜"

Front (right side)

¼" to ⅜"

Fold ends in

Front (right side)

Gold thread

Front (right side)

Figure 6

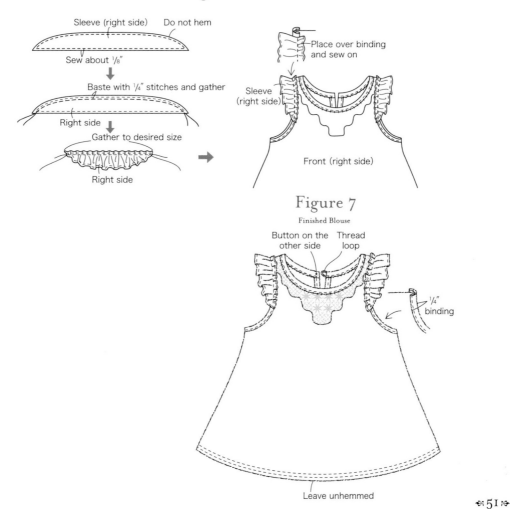

Sleeve (right side)   Do not hem

Sew about ⅛"

Baste with ¼" stitches and gather

Right side

Gather to desired size

Right side

Place over binding and sew on

Sleeve (right side)

Front (right side)

Figure 7

Finished Blouse

Button on the other side   Thread loop

¼" binding

Leave unhemmed

Natural Cotton Skirt

Photograph on page 15.

Finished Measurements (for sizes 4, 5, 6, and 7, respectively)

Waist: 23⅝", 24⅜", 25¼", 26"
Hip: 23⅝", 25¼", 26¾", 28⅜"
Skirt length: 16", 17⅛", 19", 20⅞"

Materials

* Pattern: 2-G from pattern insert (3 pattern pieces)
* Fabric A: Thick cotton, 43¼" wide. For sizes 4 and 5: 23⅝"; for sizes 6 and 7: 27½"
* Fabric B: Sheeting, 35½" wide. For sizes 4 and 5: 23⅝"; for sizes 6 and 7: 31½"
* Fabric C: Indian cotton, 27½" wide. For sizes 4 and 5: 39⅜"; for sizes 6 and 7: 67"
* Cotton tape: ¼" × 67"
* Eye hooks: 3 large

Instructions

1. **Cut out the pattern pieces.** Following pattern 2-G in the back of the book, and referring to Figure 1, trace the patterns for the top, middle, and bottom skirts; the yoke; and the facing onto a separate sheet of paper.
2. **Cut fabric A.** Fold over both ends of fabric A, selvage to selvage, right sides together. Position the pattern pieces for the top skirt (front and back) and yoke (front and back) as shown in Figure 2. Add seam allowances to the fabric as shown before cutting it.
3. **Cut fabric B.** Fold fabric B in half, selvage to selvage, right sides together. Position the pattern pieces for the skirt middle front and back, as shown in Figure 3. Add seam allowances to the fabric as shown before cutting it.
4. **Cut fabric C.** Fold fabric C in half, selvage to selvage, right sides together, and position the pattern pieces for the skirt bottom, yoke, and facing as shown in Figure 4. Add seam allowances to the fabric as shown before cutting it. Cut the ruffle to the measurements shown.
5. **Sew each skirt.** Starting with the bottom skirt, place the front on the back, right sides together. Sew along both sides, being sure to leave an opening on the top of the left side for the skirt opening. Finish the edges with a zigzag stitch. Repeat for the middle and top skirts. *See Figure 5.*
6. **Create gathers.** Create gathers in the bottom and middle skirts either by hand or by making longer stitches on your machine. Gather the layers along the top edge, in proportion to the measurements of the yoke.
7. **Attach the skirts.** Layer the three skirts inside one another, right sides up. Sew or baste the top three edges together.
8. **Sew the yokes.** Fabric A is the outside yoke and fabric C is the inside yoke. Place the fabric A yoke back on the fabric A yoke front, right sides together. Sew along one short side and press. Fold under the seam allowances of the sides and the waist and press. Repeat for the fabric C yoke. *See Figure 6.*
9. **Attach the skirt to the yoke.** Place the two yokes right sides together. Place the skirt in between the yokes so the right side of the skirt is facing the right side of the outside yoke. Stitch along the top edge, being sure to leave

an opening along the left side of the skirt. *See Figure 7.*

10. **Finish the yoke.** Turn the yokes right side out. Stitch around the top of the yolk five times to strengthen the waist. Stitch two or three times around the skirt opening to reinforce it, leaving a gap at the top of the skirt for the tie to feed through. *See Figure 8.*

11. **Attach the facing.** Fold the facing fabric in half, and place it over the rear left side of the skirt opening. Stitch it in place. *See Figure 9.*

12. **Attach the closures.** Attach the eye hooks to the opening. Pass the cotton tape through the waist to serve as a tie. *See Figure 10.*

13. **Finish the skirt.** Gather the ruffle, and attach it to the left hem of the bottom skirt. Place it wherever it seems to be in balance with the rest of the skirt. *See Figure 11.*

Figure 1

Pattern Details for 2-G

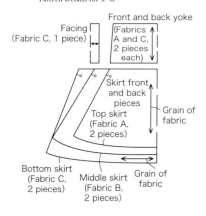

Figure 2

Skirt Layout: Fabric A

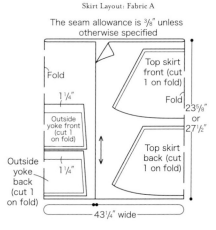

Figure 3

Skirt Layout: Fabric B

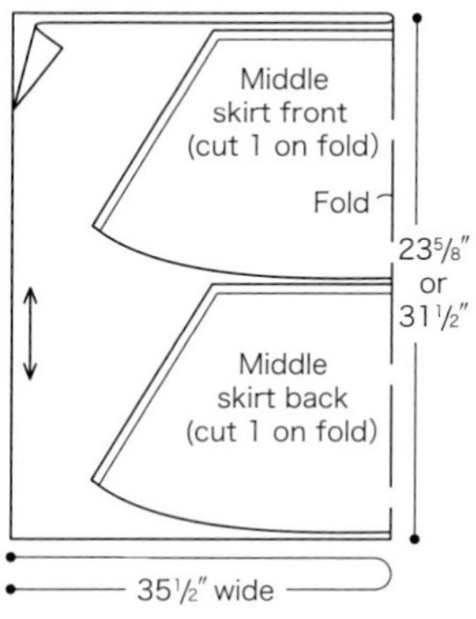

Figure 4

Skirt Layout: Fabric C

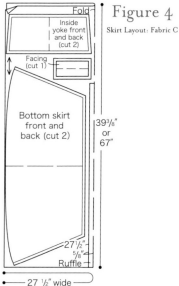

Figure 5

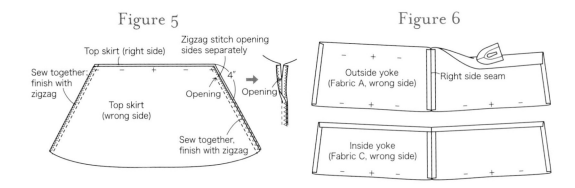

Top skirt (right side)

Zigzag stitch opening sides separately

Sew together; finish with zigzag

4"

Opening

Opening

Top skirt (wrong side)

Sew together, finish with zigzag

Opening

Figure 6

Outside yoke (Fabric A, wrong side)

Right side seam

Inside yoke (Fabric C, wrong side)

Figure 7

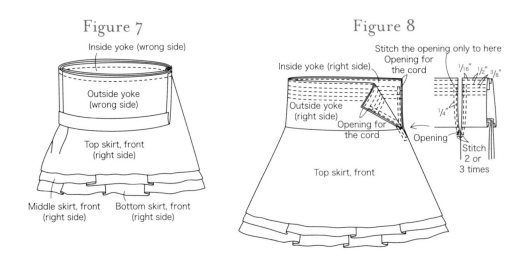

Inside yoke (wrong side)

Outside yoke (wrong side)

Top skirt, front (right side)

Middle skirt, front (right side)

Bottom skirt, front (right side)

Figure 8

Stitch the opening only to here

Opening for the cord

Inside yoke (right side)

Outside yoke (right side)

Opening for the cord

Opening

$\frac{1}{16}$" $\frac{1}{2}$" $\frac{3}{8}$"

$\frac{1}{4}$"

Stitch 2 or 3 times

Top skirt, front

Figure 9

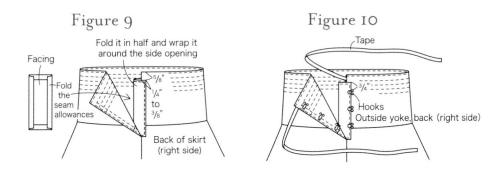

Facing

Fold the seam allowances

Fold it in half and wrap it around the side opening

5/8"

1/4" to 3/8"

Back of skirt (right side)

Figure 10

Tape

3/4"

Hooks

Outside yoke, back (right side)

Figure 11

Finished Skirt

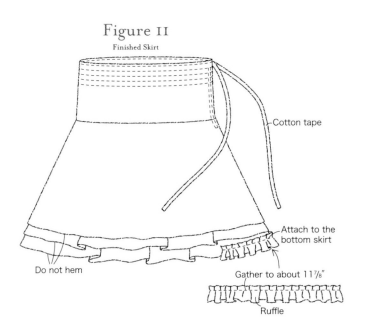

Cotton tape

Attach to the bottom skirt

Do not hem

Gather to about 11 7/8"

Ruffle

Bag

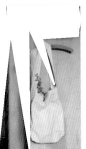

Photograph on page 16.

Finished Measurements (one size)

$13\frac{3}{8}$" × $15\frac{3}{4}$"

Materials

* Pattern: No pattern necessary
* Outer fabric: Sailcloth, $35\frac{1}{2}$" wide × $27\frac{1}{2}$"
* Lining: Thin sheeting, $29\frac{1}{2}$" × $19\frac{3}{4}$"
* Lace doily: 1
* Leather tape: $\frac{3}{8}$" × 4"
* Button: 1, $\frac{5}{8}$" in diameter

Instructions

1. **Cut the fabric.** Following the measurements in Figure 1, cut the fabric pieces from the outer fabric and lining. Add a seam allowance to the fabric before cutting it.
2. **Attach the doily.** Place a lace doily to one side of the bag so that it is in balance with the rest of the bag. Hand stitch it in place. *See Figure 2.*
3. **Sew the outer fabric to the lining.** Place the outer fabric of the bag front on the lining for the bag front, right sides together. Stitch along three sides, $\frac{3}{8}$" from the edge. Turn right side out. Repeat for the bag back. Place the bag front on the bag back, right sides of the outer fabric together. Stitch along all three sides, and turn the bag right side out. *See Figure 3.*
4. **Sew the bag top and corners.** Fold the outer fabric and lining of the bag top separately by $2\frac{3}{8}$" toward the wrong side. The raw edges of the bag top are now between the outer fabric and the lining. Stitch around the bag top. Form gussets by flattening the bottom corners of the bag to a width of $3\frac{1}{8}$". Stitch across the corner, fold it over, and hand stitch it in place. *See Figure 4.*
5. **Add the handles.** Place the two pieces of fabric for the handles together, wrong sides facing each other. Stitch in rows down the length of the handle. Stitch the ends of the handle to opposite sides of the bag, centered over the side seams. Place the button at the midpoint of the opening, and hand stitch the piece of leather with a buttonhole cut in it to the opposite side. *See Figure 5.*

Figure 1

Bag Layout: Outer Fabric

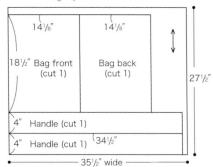

$14\frac{1}{8}$" $14\frac{1}{8}$"

$18\frac{1}{2}$" Bag front (cut 1) Bag back (cut 1) $27\frac{1}{2}$"

4" Handle (cut 1)

4" Handle (cut 1) $34\frac{1}{2}$"

$35\frac{1}{2}$" wide

Bag Layout: Lining

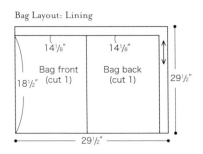

$14\frac{1}{8}$" $14\frac{1}{8}$"

$18\frac{1}{2}$" Bag front (cut 1) Bag back (cut 1) $29\frac{1}{2}$"

$29\frac{1}{2}$"

Figure 2

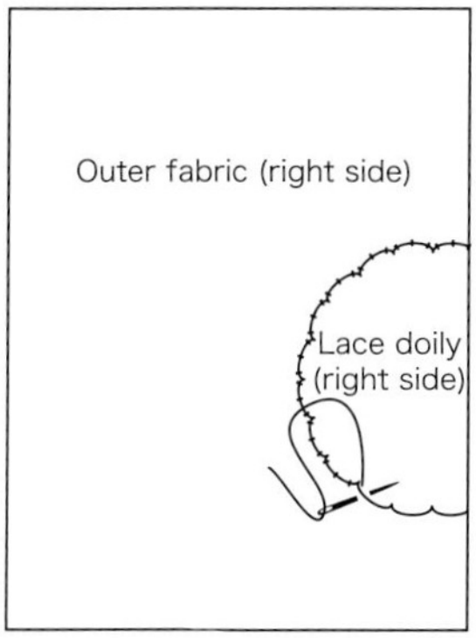

Outer fabric (right side)

Lace doily (right side)

Figure 3

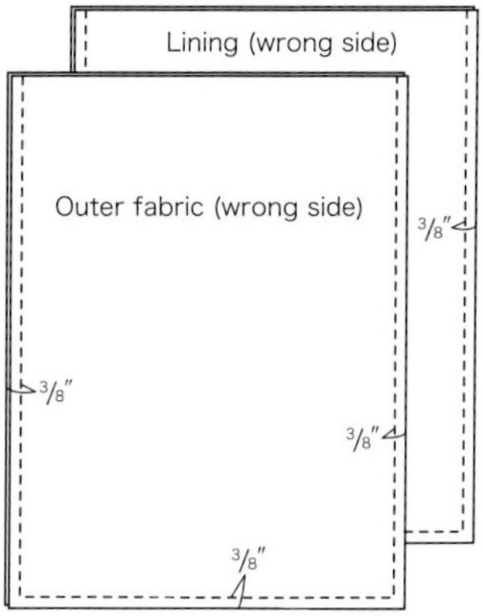

Lining (wrong side)

Outer fabric (wrong side)

3/8"

3/8"

3/8"

3/8"

Figure 4

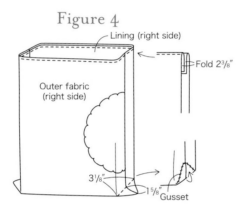

Lining (right side)

Fold 2³/₈"

Outer fabric (right side)

3¹/₈"

1⁵/₈" Gusset

Figure 5

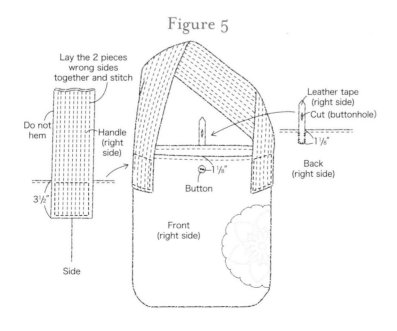

Lay the 2 pieces wrong sides together and stitch

Do not hem

Handle (right side)

3¹/₂"

Side

Leather tape (right side)

Cut (buttonhole)

1¹/₈"

Back (right side)

Button

1¹/₈"

Front (right side)

Black Linen Hat

Photograph on page 23.

Finished Measurements (for sizes Small, Medium, and Large)

Head circumference: $20\frac{7}{8}$", $21\frac{5}{8}$", $22\frac{1}{2}$"

Materials

* Pattern: 2-D from pattern insert (4 pattern pieces)
* Fabric: Linen, $37\frac{3}{8}$" × $15\frac{3}{4}$"
* Lace: 4 or 5 kinds, in any amount
* Button: 1, $\frac{5}{8}$" in diameter
* Embroidery floss: Gold, as needed

Instructions

1. **Cut out the pattern pieces.** Following pattern 2-D in the back of the book, and referring to Figure 1, trace the patterns for the top crown, the side crown (top), the side crown (bottom), and the brim onto a separate sheet of paper.

2. **Cut the fabric.** Fold over one end of the fabric, selvage to selvage, right sides together. Position the pattern as shown in Figure 2. Add a seam allowance to the fabric before cutting it.

3. **Make the top crown.** Place the two top crown pieces together, right sides facing up, and zigzag stitch around the edge three times, being sure to stay within the seam allowance. *See Figure 3.*

4. **Attach the side crowns.** Finish the sides of the side crown fabrics with a zigzag stitch to prevent fraying. Place the top side crown on the bottom side crown, right sides together, and stitch in place along the bottom edge. Open and press the seam allowances down; stitch them in place using a zigzag stitch. *See Figure 4.*

5. **Attach the crown top to the sides.** Fold the side crown in half, right sides together, and stitch the short edges in place to create a circle. Finish the edge of the top crown with a zigzag stitch. Place the right side of the top crown on the wrong side of the side crown. Stitch around the top of the hat, securing the top crown to the side crown. Turn the hat right side out. *See Figure 5.*

6. **Make the brim.** Place the two pieces for the outer brim right sides together. Sew along the two short sides and press the seams open. Repeat for the inner brim. Place the outer brim over the inner brim, right sides together, and stitch around the bottom. Turn the brim right side out. *See Figure 6.*

7. **Attach the brim to the crown sides.** Place the brim over the crown sides by $\frac{3}{8}$", and zigzag stitch in place all the way around the hat. *See Figure 7.*

8. **Finish the hat.** Hand embroider decorative running stitches with the gold thread. Position the lace as you like, in a balanced manner, along the line where the brim is attached. Sew the lace in place, and attach a button. *See Figure 8.*

Figure 1

Pattern Details for 2-D

Top crown

Side crown, top

Side crown, bottom

Brim

Figure 2

Hat Layout

The seam allowance is $^3/_8$"

Fold

Cut about $^1/_4$" smaller

Side crown, top
(cut 2)

Side crown, bottom
(cut 2)

Outer brim
(cut 2)

Inner brim
(cut 2)

Top
crown,
(cut 1)

Top
crown,
(cut 1)

15$^3/_4$"

37$^3/_8$"

Figure 3

Cut edge is unhemmed

Top crown
(right side)

Zigzag
stitch

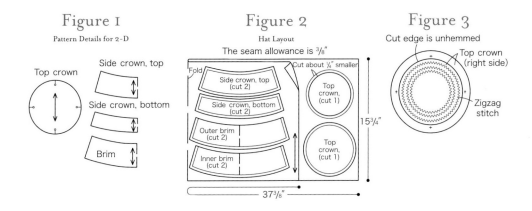

Figure 4

Wrong
side

Side crown, top
(right side)

Side crown, bottom
(right side)

Zigzag stitch

Figure 5

Top crown (wrong side)

Side crown
(wrong side)

Zigzag stitch
the two pieces
together

Side

Figure 6

Brim (wrong side)

Press seam
open

Side crown, bottom
(wrong side)

Side crown,
top (right side)

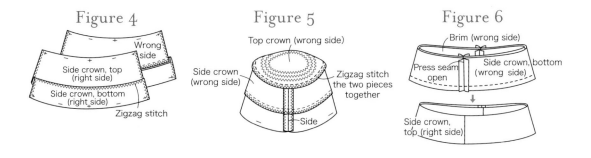

Figure 7

Crown

Right side

Brim (right side)

Do not hem

Lay the brim on and zigzag stitch

Figure 8

Hand stitch

Side

Lace

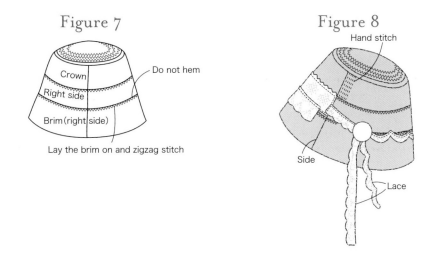

Dress with Lace Doily

Photograph on page 19.

Finished Measurements (for sizes 4, 5, 6, and 7, respectively)

Chest: 26¾", 28⅜", 30", 31½"
Length (from the shoulders): 24⅜",
   26¼", 28⅛", 30¼"
Sleeve length: 5½", 6⅛", 6⅞", 7¾"

Materials

* Pattern: 1-A from pattern insert
  (3 pattern pieces)
* Fabric: Indian cotton, 59½" wide. For
  sizes 4 and 5: 35½". For sizes 6 and 7:
  43⅜"
* Lace doily: 1
* Button: 1, ⅝" in diameter
* Lace thread, as needed

Instructions

1. **Cut out the pattern pieces.** Following pattern 1-A in the back of the book, and referring to Figure 1, trace the patterns for the dress back, dress front, and sleeve onto a separate sheet of paper.
2. **Cut the fabric.** Fold the fabric in half, selvage to selvage, right sides together. Position the pattern as shown in Figure 2. Add a seam allowance to the fabric before cutting it. Cut the bias binding 45° to the fabric grain to the exact measurements shown.
3. **Sew the dress front.** Finish the shoulders, sides, and bottom of the dress front with zigzag stitches to prevent fraying. Determine the appropriate position of the lace doily based on its size and how it looks with the other elements. Cut off one edge of the round doily, and set it aside to use around the collar. Align the cut edge with the edge of the dress front. Machine stitch and hand stitch the doily in place. *See Figure 4.*
4. **Sew the dress back.** Finish the shoulders, sides, and bottom of the two dress back pieces with zigzag stitches to prevent fraying. Place the two back pieces right sides together. Sew down the center back, stopping at the bottom of the back opening. Press the seams open, and stitch around the back opening. (See Figure 3 on page 50.)
5. **Attach dress front to back.** Place the dress back on the front, right sides together. Sew along the shoulders and press the seam open. *See Figure 4.*
6. **Finish the neckline.** Place the cut piece of lace along the neckline as shown in Figure 4. Machine stitch it in place close to the edge. Attach the bias binding to the neckline, following the instructions on page 49. Hand stitch around the neckline on just the doily using the gold embroidery thread. *See Figure 4.*
7. **Finish sewing the dress front and back.** With the front and back right sides together, sew along the sides and press the seams open. Fold under the hem, and stitch it in place.
8. **Make the sleeves.** Finish the long edge of the sleeve with a zigzag stitch to prevent fraying. Fold the sleeve in half, right sides together, and stitch in place along the short side. Press the seam open, fold under the hem, and stitch it in place. Baste along the top edge of the sleeve. Pull the ends of the thread to gather the fabric, referring to the markings from the pattern. *See Figure 5.*
9. **Attach the sleeves.** With the dress

wrong side out, place the sleeves inside the dress, aligning the edges and placing the pieces right sides together. Stitch the sleeves in place around the armholes. Finish the seam with a zigzag stitch through both seam allowances. Fold the seam allowance under, toward the sleeve. Turn the dress right side out. *See Figure 6.*

10. **Finish the dress.** Make a thread loop following the instructions on page 68. Attach the loop to the back opening, and sew the button on the opposite side. *See Figure 7.*

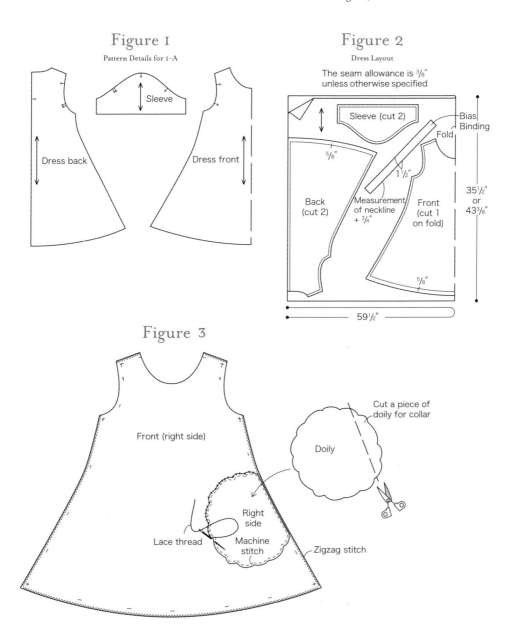

Figure 1
Pattern Details for 1-A

Sleeve

Dress back

Dress front

Figure 2
Dress Layout

The seam allowance is ³/₈" unless otherwise specified

Sleeve (cut 2)

Bias Binding

Fold

⁵/₈"

1½"

Back (cut 2)

Measurement of neckline + ³/₄"

Front (cut 1 on fold)

35½" or 43³/₈"

⁵/₈"

59½"

Figure 3

Front (right side)

Cut a piece of doily for collar

Doily

Right side

Lace thread

Machine stitch

Zigzag stitch

Figure 4

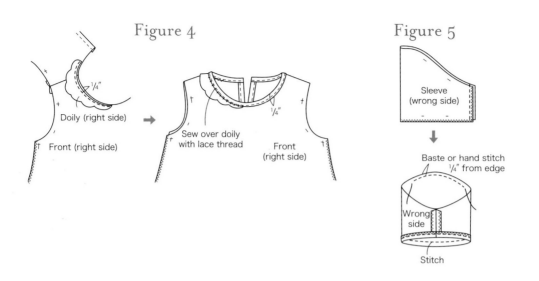

¼"

Doily (right side)

Front (right side)

Sew over doily
with lace thread

¼"

Front
(right side)

Figure 5

Sleeve
(wrong side)

Baste or hand stitch
¼" from edge

Wrong
side

Stitch

Figure 6

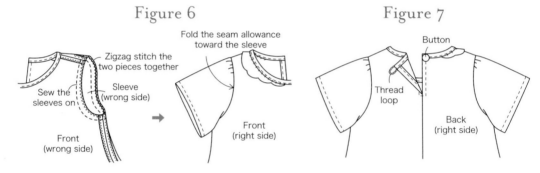

Zigzag stitch the
two pieces together

Sew the
sleeves on

Sleeve
(wrong side)

Front
(wrong side)

Fold the seam allowance
toward the sleeve

Front
(right side)

Figure 7

Button

Thread
loop

Back
(right side)

Figure 8

Finished Dress

White Cotton and Flower Print Sundress

Photograph on page 21.

Finished Measurements (for sizes 4, 5, 6, and 7, respectively)

Chest: 22", 23⅝", 25¼", 26¾"
Length (from the shoulders): 26⅜", 28⅛", 30", 31⅝"

Materials

* Pattern: I–C from pattern insert (2 pattern pieces)
* Fabric A: White cotton. For sizes 4 and 5: 31½" × 9⅞"; for sizes 6 and 7: 33½" × 11⅞"
* Fabric B: Indian cotton, 59⅛" wide. For sizes 4 and 5: 19¾"; for sizes 6 and 7: 23⅝"
* Lining (bodice): Gauze. For sizes 4 and 5: 31½" × 9⅞"; for sizes 6 and 7: 33½" × 11⅞"
* Fabric scraps: Two types of cotton, any amount
* Lace: ⅞" wide. For sizes 4 and 5: 51 ½"; for sizes 6 and 7: 54⅛"
* Buttons: 3, ½" in diameter; 1, ⅝" in diameter
* Silver thread: Metallic sewing machine thread, as needed

Instructions

1. **Cut out the pattern pieces.** Following pattern I–C in the back of the book, and referring to Figure 1, trace the patterns for the bodice front and the bodice back onto a separate sheet of paper. Note the measurements for the skirt and the pocket; no patterns are needed for these pieces.
2. **Cut the fabric.** Fold fabric B in half, selvage to selvage, right sides together. Cut the skirt and the pocket to the measurements shown in Figure 1. Fold fabric A, selvage to selvage, right sides together; fold the lining the same way. Lay fabric A on top of the lining. Position the pattern as shown in Figure 2. Add a seam allowance to the fabric before cutting it.
3. **Attach bodice front to bodice back.** Place the bodice front on the bodice back, right sides together. Sew along the shoulder, and press the seams open. Repeat for the bodice lining. *See Figure 3.*
4. **Attach the lining to the bodice.** Place the bodice on the lining, right sides together. Sew along the back opening and the inside neck, and then sew the armholes. Clip into the seam allowance of the curves in the armhole and the corners along the inside neck. Turn the bodice right side out. Press the seams, and add decorative hand stitching to the front neckline. *See Figure 3.*
5. **Sew the side seams.** Fold the bodice inside out, with right sides together. Sew along the side seams of the bodice front and back, and then sew along the side seams of the lining front and back. Turn the bodice right side out, and sew around the armholes. *See Figure 4.*
6. **Make the pocket.** Using the fabric scraps, create a pleasing patchwork for the pocket. Cut the patchwork to the measurements given in Figure 1. Fold under the top of the pocket twice, and stitch. Press the side seam allowance toward the wrong side. Position the pocket on the skirt front, and stitch it in place. Use a zigzag stitch around the edge of the pocket. *See Figure 5.*
7. **Make the skirt.** Place the skirt front

on the skirt back, right sides together, and sew along the two sides. Press the seams open. Fold the seam allowance of the hem under, toward the wrong side. Place the lace on the right side of the skirt along the bottom edge. Sew around the skirt bottom with the silver thread, securing the hem and the lace.

8. **Attach the skirt to the bodice.** Baste around the top edge of the skirt. Pull the ends of the thread to gather the fabric to the same measurement as the bottom edge of the bodice. Place the gathered skirt inside the bodice, right sides together. Sew around the top edge. Use a zigzag stitch through the three layers to finish the seam.

9. **Finish the dress.** Make four thread loops following the instructions on page 68. Attach the loops to the back opening and sew the buttons on the opposite side. *See Figure 6.*

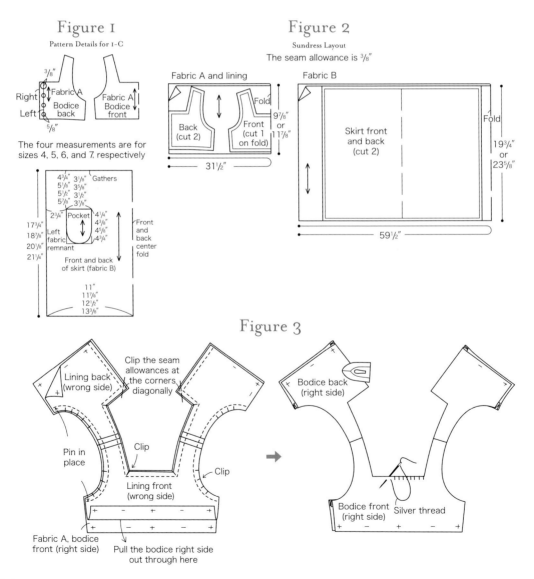

Figure 1

Pattern Details for 1-C

The four measurements are for sizes 4, 5, 6, and 7, respectively

Figure 2

Sundress Layout
The seam allowance is 3/8"

Figure 3

Figure 4

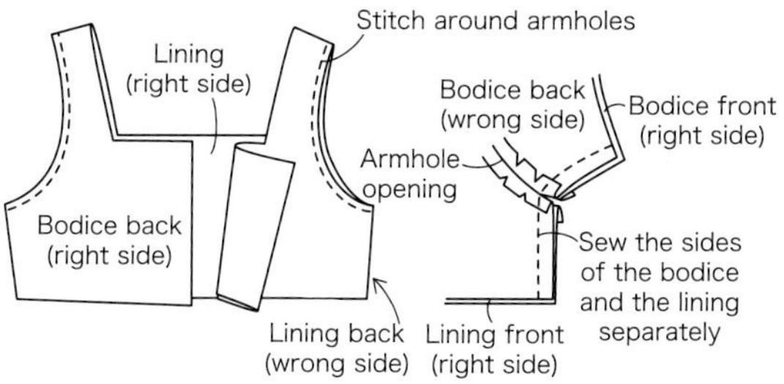

Lining (right side)

Stitch around armholes

Bodice back (right side)

Bodice back (wrong side)

Bodice front (right side)

Armhole opening

Lining back (wrong side)

Lining front (right side)

Sew the sides of the bodice and the lining separately

Figure 5

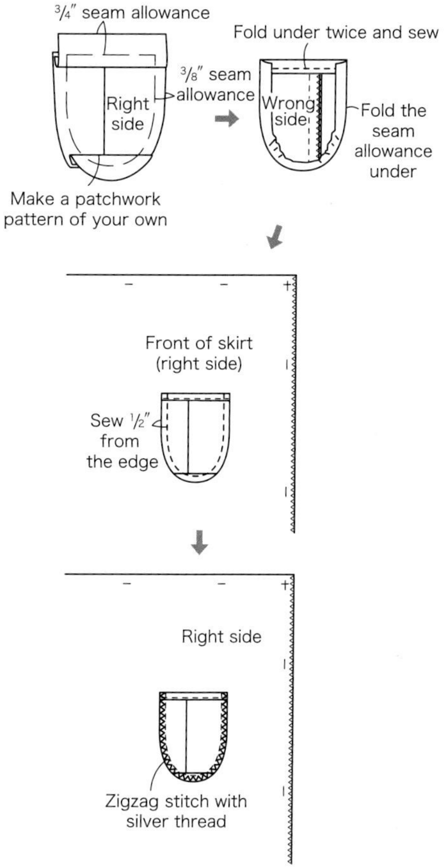

$3/4$" seam allowance

Fold under twice and sew

$3/8$" seam allowance

Right side

Wrong side

Fold the seam allowance under

Make a patchwork pattern of your own

− − +

Front of skirt (right side)

Sew $1/2$" from the edge

− − +

Right side

Zigzag stitch with silver thread

Figure 6

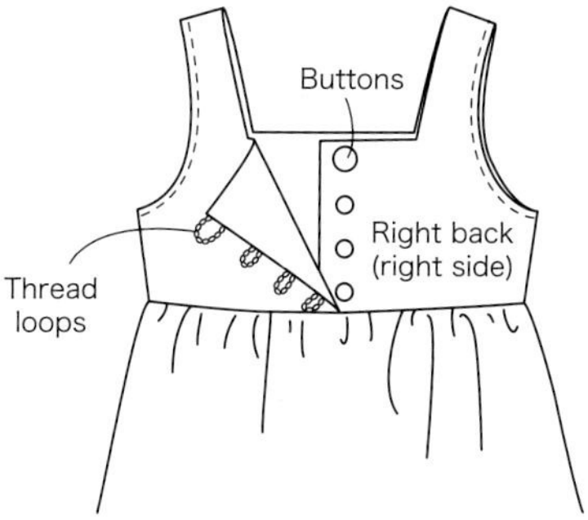

Buttons

Right back (right side)

Thread loops

Figure 7

Finished Sundress

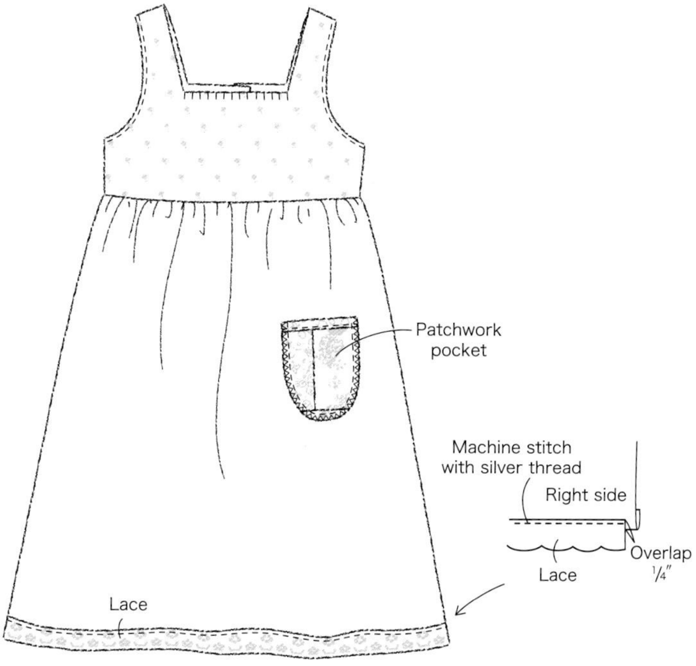

Patchwork pocket

Machine stitch with silver thread

Right side

Overlap $1/4$"

Lace

Lace

Chemise

Photograph on page 22.

Finished Measurements (for sizes 4, 5, 6, and 7, respectively)

Chest: 24⅜", 26", 27½", 29⅛"
Length: 16⅞", 18⅛", 19⅜", 20½"

Materials

* Pattern: 1-A from pattern insert (2 pattern pieces)
* Fabric: Gauze, 59½" × 25⅝"
* Lace: ¼" wide. For sizes 4 and 5: 86⅝"; for sizes 6 and 7: 98½"
* Buttons: 3, ¼" in diameter; 1, ½" in diameter
* Silver thread: Metallic machine thread, as needed

Instructions

1. **Cut out the pattern pieces.** Following pattern 1-A in the back of the book, and referring to Figure 1, trace the patterns for the dress front and back onto a separate sheet of paper. Adjust the pattern for the chemise as follows: Use the neckline and armholes from the bodice back just as they are; draw new lines for the side seam, cutting in ⅝" at the start of the armhole. Draw new hem lines for the back to the measurements shown. On the bodice front, enlarge the neckline by dropping the center point 1¼"; use the shoulders and armholes as is. Draw new side seams for the front, cutting in ⅝" at the start of the armhole; draw new side seams the same length as the back side seams.

2. **Cut the fabric.** Fold the fabric in half, selvage to selvage, right sides together. Position the pattern as shown in Figure 2. Add a seam allowance to the fabric before cutting it.

3. **Sew the back.** Zigzag stitch around the sides, armholes, neck, and middle back to prevent fraying. Place the two back pieces right sides together. Sew up the center back, stopping at the bottom of the back opening. Press the seams open, and stitch around the back opening. (See Figure 3 on page 50.)

4. **Attach the bodice front to the back.** Place the bodice back on the bodice front, right sides together. Sew along the shoulders, and press the seams open. *See Figure 3.*

5. **Finish the neck and armholes.** Fold the seam allowances of the neckline and armholes under, toward the wrong side, and press. Lay the lace around the right side of the neckline, and stitch it in place. *See Figure 3.*

6. **Sew the side seams.** With the bodice front and back right sides together, sew along the side seams. Press the seam open. *See Figure 4.*

7. **Hem the chemise.** Fold the hem under twice toward the wrong side and stitch it in place. *See Figure 5.*

8. **Finish the chemise.** Sew lace around the armholes, and hem. Sew three decorative buttons onto the front center, and hand stitch six lines of decorative running stitches from the front neckline with silver thread. Make a thread loop following the instructions in Figure 6. Attach the loop to the back opening and sew the button on the opposite side. *See Figure 6.*

Figure 1

Pattern Details for Adapting 1-A

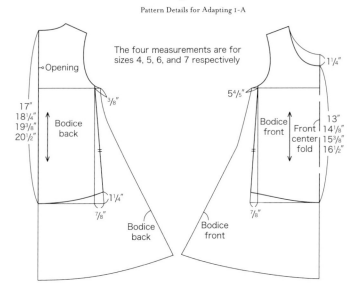

The four measurements are for sizes 4, 5, 6, and 7 respectively

Opening

17"
18¼"
19⅜"
20½"

Bodice back

³⁄₈"

1¼"

⁷⁄₈"

Bodice back

1¼"

5⁴⁄₅"

Bodice front

Front center fold

13"
14⅛"
15⅜"
16½"

⁷⁄₈"

Bodice front

Figure 2

Chemise Layout

The seam allowance is ³⁄₈" unless otherwise specified

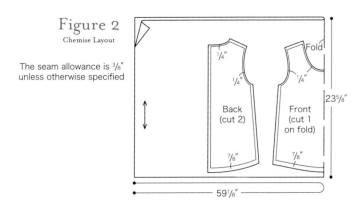

¼"

¼"

Back (cut 2)

Fold

¼"

¼"

Front (cut 1 on fold)

23⁵⁄₈"

⁷⁄₈"

⁷⁄₈"

59⅛"

Figure 3

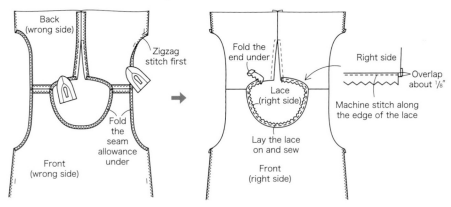

Back (wrong side)

Zigzag stitch first

Fold the seam allowance under

Front (wrong side)

Fold the end under

Lace (right side)

Lay the lace on and sew

Front (right side)

Right side

Overlap about ⅛"

Machine stitch along the edge of the lace

Figure 4

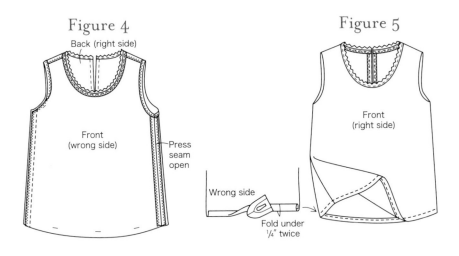

Back (right side)

Front
(wrong side)

Press
seam
open

Figure 5

Front
(right side)

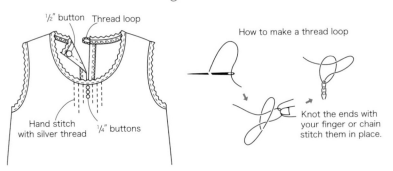

Wrong side

Fold under
¼" twice

Figure 6

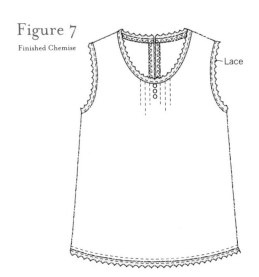

½" button   Thread loop

Hand stitch
with silver thread   ¼" buttons

How to make a thread loop

Knot the ends with
your finger or chain
stitch them in place.

Figure 7

Finished Chemise

Lace

Dress with Quilted Bodice

Photograph on page 24.

Finished Measurements (for sizes 4, 5, 6, and 7, respectively)

Chest: 22⅞", 23⅝", 25¼", 26¾"
Length: 27¾", 29½", 31¼", 33"

Materials

* Pattern: I-B and I-C from pattern insert (3 pattern pieces)
* Outer fabric: Cotton/linen double gauze, 42½" wide. For sizes 4 and 5: 39⅜"; for sizes 6 and 7: 55⅛"
* Contrasting fabric: Cotton gauze, 59⅛" wide. For sizes 4 and 5: 31½"; for sizes 6 and 7: 35½"
* Lining: Thin sheeting, 35⅞" × 11⅞"
* Quilt batting: 35½" × 11⅞"
* Buttons: 1, ⅝" in diameter; 3, ½" in diameter
* Embroidery floss: Gold, as needed

Instructions

1. **Cut out the pattern pieces.** Following pattern I-B in the back of the book, and referring to Figure 1, trace the pattern for the sleeve ruffle onto a separate sheet of paper. Following the pattern for I-C in the back of the book, and referring to Figure 1, trace the pattern for the bodice front and bodice back onto a separate sheet of paper. Note the measurements for the skirt and hem ruffles; no patterns are necessary for these pieces.

2. **Cut the fabric.** Fold the edges of the outer fabric in, selvage to selvage, right sides together. Position the pattern as shown in Figure 2. Add a seam allowance to the fabric before cutting it. Fold the lining fabric in half, selvage to selvage, right sides together. Position the patterns for the bodice back and bodice front as shown in Figure 3. Note the measurements for the facing in Figure 1. Add a seam allowance to the fabric before cutting it. Fold the contrasting fabric in half, selvage to selvage, right sides together, and position the sleeve ruffle pattern as shown in Figure 4. Note the measurements for the skirt (see Figure 1) and hem ruffles. Add a seam allowance to the fabric before cutting it.

3. **Quilt the bodice front.** Cut the quilt batting to the same size as the bodice front and bodice back. Place the quilt batting on the wrong side of the outer bodice front. Stitch the batting in place around the outline of the bodice front, close to the edge. Hand quilt the pieces together in rows as shown. Repeat the same process with the outer bodice back. *See Figure 5.*

4. **Attach the bodice back to the front.** Place the two quilted bodice back pieces on the quilted bodice front, right sides together. Sew up the side seams and press the seam allowance open. Repeat for the lining bodice back and bodice front.

5. **Attach the lining to the bodice.** Lay the quilted bodice on the bodice lining, right sides together. Backstitch around the armholes, the front neckline, and the back neckline. Clip the seam allowances along the curves, being careful not to cut into the seams. Turn the bodice right side out. Fold the edges of the facing under ⅜" on all sides. Wrap it around one edge

of the back opening. Stitch it in place. *See Figure 6.*

6. **Sew the shoulder seams.** Fold the bodice so the outer fabric is to the inside. Move the lining of the shoulders away, and stitch the shoulder seams of the outer fabric. Fold the shoulder seams of the lining under and hem them by hand. *See Figure 7.*

7. **Attach the ruffles to the armholes.** Make the ruffle sleeves and sew them to the dress following the instructions on page 50.

8. **Sew the outer skirt.** With the right sides together, stitch the side seams of the outer skirt and stitch around the hem to prevent fraying. Finish the seam allowances of the side seams with a zigzag stitch.

9. **Sew the contrasting fabric skirt.** With the right sides together, stitch the side seams of the contrasting fabric skirt. Lay the hem ruffle pieces together, and stitch the short ends together to form a circle. Set your sewing machine to a long stitch, and sew around the entire circle ⅝" from the upper edge. Pull the threads to gather the ruffles to match the bottom edge of the skirt. Lay wrong side of the ruffles on the right side of the contrasting skirt. Sew the ruffles to the bottom of the contrasting fabric skirt. *See Figure 8.*

10. **Gather the waist.** Set your sewing machine to a long stitch, and sew around the top of the outer skirt, ⅜" from the top edge. Repeat on the contrasting fabric skirt. Slip the outer skirt over the contrasting fabric skirt, right sides fac-

ing out. Pull the threads to gather the waists of both skirts to match the bottom edge of the bodice. *See Figure 8.*

11. **Join the skirts and the bodice.** Fit the skirt over the bodice, with the right side of the bodice facing the wrong side of the skirts. Machine stitch over the gathers. *See Figure 8.*

12. **Finish the dress.** Hand stitch around the neckline with gold thread. Make four thread loops following the instructions on page 68. Attach the loops to the back opening. Sew the ⅝" button at the top of the back opening along the facing, and place the other buttons below it and opposite the other three thread loops. *See Figure 9.*

Figure I

Pattern Details for 1-B and 1-C

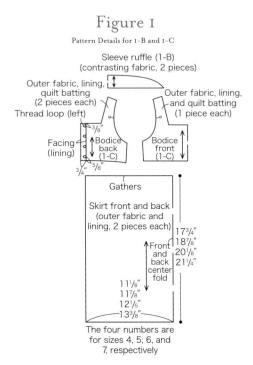

Sleeve ruffle (1-B)
(contrasting fabric, 2 pieces)

Outer fabric, lining,
quilt batting
(2 pieces each)

Thread loop (left)

Outer fabric, lining,
and quilt batting
(1 piece each)

Facing
(lining)

3/8"

Bodice
back
(1-C)

Bodice
front
(1-C)

3/4"   5/8"

Gathers

Skirt front and back
(outer fabric and
lining, 2 pieces each)

17¾"
18⅞"
20⅛"
21¼"

Front
and
back
center
fold

11⅛"
11⅞"
12⅕"
13⅜"

The four numbers are
for sizes 4, 5, 6, and
7, respectively

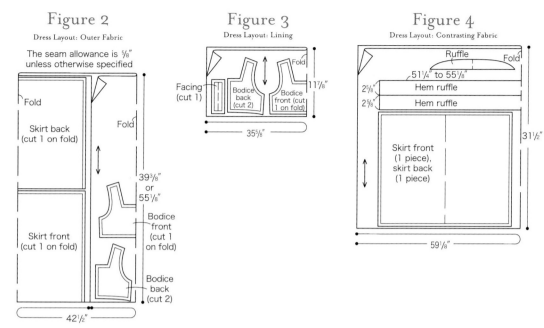

Figure 2

Dress Layout: Outer Fabric

Figure 3

Dress Layout: Lining

Figure 4

Dress Layout: Contrasting Fabric

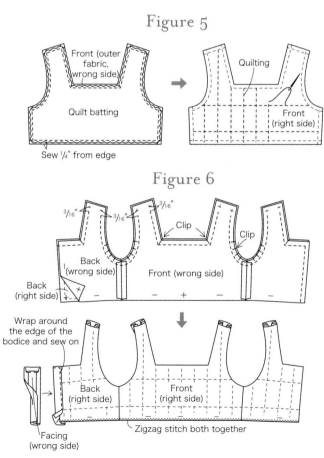

Figure 5

Figure 6

Figure 7

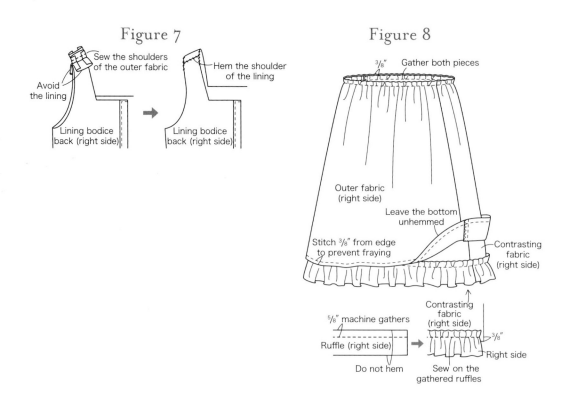

Sew the shoulders of the outer fabric

Avoid the lining

Hem the shoulder of the lining

Lining bodice back (right side)

Lining bodice back (right side)

Figure 8

Gather both pieces

3/8"

Outer fabric (right side)

Leave the bottom unhemmed

Stitch 3/8" from edge to prevent fraying

Contrasting fabric (right side)

Contrasting fabric (right side)

5/8" machine gathers

Ruffle (right side)

Do not hem

3/8"

Right side

Sew on the gathered ruffles

Figure 9

Finished Dress

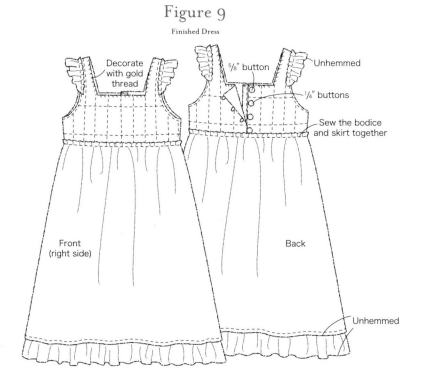

Decorate with gold thread

Unhemmed

5/8" button

1/4" buttons

Sew the bodice and skirt together

Front (right side)

Back

Unhemmed

Crossover Tunic

Photograph on page 26.

Finished Measurements (for sizes 4, 5, 6, and 7, respectively)

Chest: 26¾", 28⅜", 30", 31½"
Length: 16¾", 18¼", 19⅝", 21½"

Materials

* Pattern: 1-E from pattern insert
  (4 pattern pieces)
* Fabric: Linen, 59" wide. For sizes 4
  and 5: 23⅝"; for sizes 6 and 7: 31½"
* Lace: 2" to 3" wide, as needed
* Linen tape: ⅜" × 70⅞" to 78¾"
* Lace thread, as needed

Note

The left side of this garment goes over the right. If you want to have the right side on top, place the left ties on the outside and the right ties on the inside.

Instructions

1. **Cut out the pattern pieces.** Following pattern 1-E in the back of the book, and referring to Figure 1, trace the patterns for the tunic front, tunic back, facing front, and facing back onto a separate sheet of paper.
2. **Cut the fabric.** Fold the fabric in half, selvage to selvage, right sides together. Position the pattern as shown in Figure 2. Add a seam allowance to the fabric before cutting it. Cut the bias binding 45° to the fabric grain to the exact measurements shown.
3. **Attach the lace to the front.** Place small pieces of lace on the shoulders

of the front bodice, and sew it in place along three sides within the seam allowance. *See Figure 3.*

4. **Attach the front bodice to the back.** Place the two back pieces on the front bodice, right sides together. Sew across the shoulders, and press the seam allowance open.
5. **Attach the facings.** Sew along the outside edge of both facings using a zigzag stitch to prevent fraying. Place the facings along the bodice neckline as shown in Figure 4, right sides together. Position two linen tape ties (17¾" to 19¾" long) as shown. Stitch the facing and ties in place. Clip inside the seam allowance along the curves. Fold the facing under to the wrong side of the bodice and press. Hand stitch around the edges of the facings with lace thread. Hand stitch the hem of the front facing. *See Figure 4.*
6. **Sew the side seams.** Place the bodice front on the bodice back, right sides together. Insert one length of linen tape (17¾" to 19¾" long) in between the front and back on the right where indicated on the side seam in Figure 6. Sew down both side seams, being sure to reinforce the tie. Press the seam allowance open.
7. **Finish the armholes.** Fold the binding fabric in half lengthwise, and press. Open the fabric and align the two short ends, right sides together. Stitch the ends together to create a circle. Fold the binding over the edges of the armholes, and stitch it in place. *See Figure 5.*
8. **Finish the tunic.** Since the bottom is not hemmed, sew along the bottom to prevent fraying. Hand stitch a length of linen tape (17¾" to 19⅗" long) to the inside seam on the left side. *See Figure 6.*

Figure 1

Pattern Details for 1-E

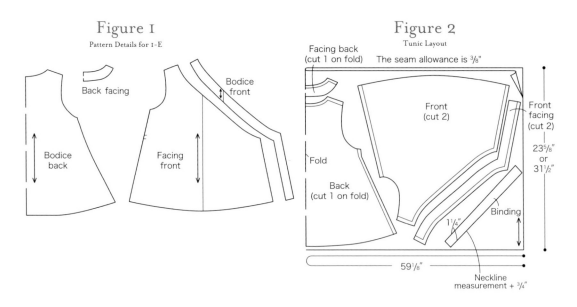

Back facing

Bodice front

Bodice back

Facing front

Figure 2

Tunic Layout

Facing back
(cut 1 on fold)

The seam allowance is $^3/_8$"

Front
(cut 2)

Front facing
(cut 2)

$23^5/_8$"
or
$31^1/_2$"

Fold

Back
(cut 1 on fold)

Binding

$1^1/_4$"

$59^1/_8$"

Neckline
measurement + $^3/_4$"

Figure 3

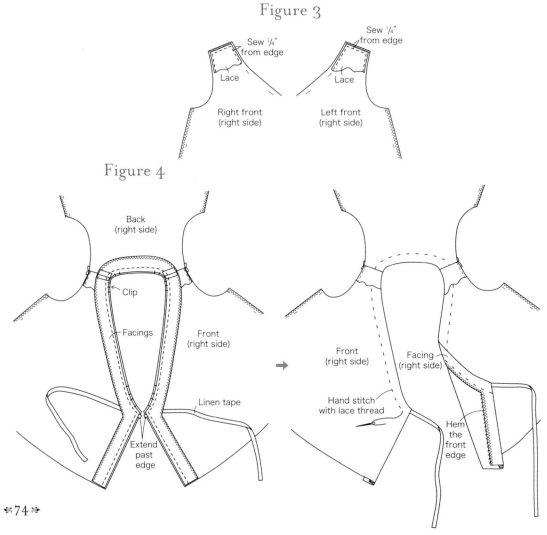

Sew $^1/_4$"
from edge

Sew $^1/_4$"
from edge

Lace

Lace

Right front
(right side)

Left front
(right side)

Figure 4

Back
(right side)

Clip

Facings

Front
(right side)

Linen tape

Extend
past
edge

Front
(right side)

Facing
(right side)

Hand stitch
with lace thread

Hem
the
front
edge

Figure 5

Binding (right side)

Leave a gap between
the edges; don't align them ↓

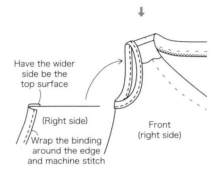

Wrong side

Leave a ⅜" seam allowance
and press it open

↓

Have the wider
side be the
top surface

(Right side)

Wrap the binding
around the edge
and machine stitch

Front
(right side)

Figure 6

Finished Tunic

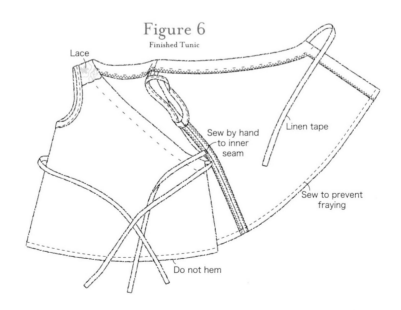

Lace

Sew by hand
to inner
seam

Linen tape

Sew to prevent
fraying

Do not hem

Dress with Ruffle Trim

Photograph on page 27.

Finished Measurements (for sizes 4, 5, 6, and 7, respectively)

Chest: 25¼", 26½", 28⅜", 30"
Length: 21", 23", 25", 27"

Materials

* Pattern: 1-B from pattern insert (4 pattern pieces)
* Outer fabric: Striped cotton, 43¼" wide. For sizes 4 and 5: 27½"; for sizes 6 and 7: 31½"
* Lining: Gauze, 59⅛" wide. For sizes 4 and 5: 31½"; for sizes 6 and 7: 35½"
* Button: 1, ½" in diameter

Instructions

1. **Cut out the pattern pieces.** Following the longer version of pattern 1-B in the back of the book, and referring to Figure 1, trace the patterns for the dress back, dress front, and sleeve onto a separate sheet of paper.
2. **Cut the fabric.** Fold the outer fabric in half, selvage to selvage, right sides together. Position the pattern as shown in Figure 2. Add a seam allowance to the fabric before cutting it. Fold the lining fabric in half, selvage to selvage, right sides together. Position the pattern as shown in Figure 3. Add a seam allowance before cutting it. Cut the bias binding 45° to the fabric grain to the exact measurements shown. Cut the hem ruffle to the measurements shown. No patterns are necessary for these pieces.
3. **Sew the back.** Place the two back pieces right sides together. Sew up the center back, stopping at the bottom of the back opening. Press the seams open. Repeat for the lining back. (See Figure 3 on page 50.)
4. **Attach the dress front and back.** Place the back on the front, right sides together, and sew across the shoulder and side seams. Press the seams open. *See Figure 4.*
5. **Finish the hem.** Do not hem the bottom of the dress. Instead, stitch around it to prevent fraying.
6. **Make the hem ruffle.** Baste along the top edge of the hem ruffle fabric. Pull the ends of the thread to gather the fabric to the length of the bottom edge of the lining front. Sew the ruffle to the hem of the lining with the right side of the ruffle against the wrong side of the lining. Repeat for the lining back. *See Figure 5.*
7. **Sew the lining back and front.** Place the lining back on the lining front, right sides together, and sew across the shoulders. Press the seams open. Turn the lining right side out.
8. **Sew the lining sides.** With the lining wrong sides together, sew the side seams together down to the ruffle. Press the seam open. *See Figure 6.*
9. **Attach the dress to the lining.** Place the dress over the lining, wrong sides together. Stitch around the back opening, the neckline, and the armholes. *See Figure 7.*
10. **Finish the neckline and the armholes.** Attach the bias binding to the neckline and armholes following the instructions on page 49.
11. **Attach the sleeves.** Make the ruffle sleeves, and sew them to the dress following the instructions on page 50.

12. **Finish the dress.** Make a thread loop following the instructions on page 68. Attach the loop to the back opening, and sew the button on the opposite side.

Figure 1
Pattern 1-B

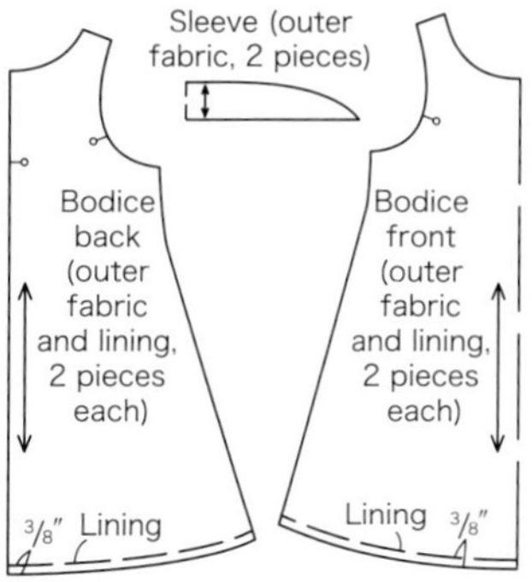

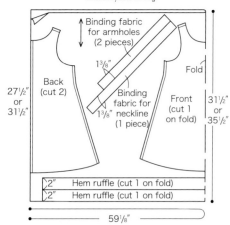

Sleeve (outer fabric, 2 pieces)

Bodice back (outer fabric and lining, 2 pieces each)

Bodice front (outer fabric and lining, 2 pieces each)

$^{3}/_{8}$" Lining

Lining $^{3}/_{8}$"

Figure 2
Dress Layout: Outer Fabric

The seam allowance is $^{3}/_{8}$"

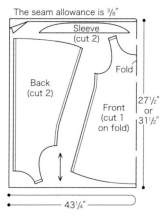

Sleeve (cut 2)

Back (cut 2)

Fold

Front (cut 1 on fold)

$27^{1}/_{2}$" or $31^{1}/_{2}$"

$43^{1}/_{4}$"

Figure 3
Dress Layout: Lining

Binding fabric for armholes (2 pieces)

Back (cut 2)

$1^{3}/_{8}$"

Fold

$27^{1}/_{2}$" or $31^{1}/_{2}$"

Binding fabric for neckline (1 piece)

$1^{3}/_{8}$"

Front (cut 1 on fold)

$31^{1}/_{2}$" or $35^{1}/_{2}$"

2" Hem ruffle (cut 1 on fold)

2" Hem ruffle (cut 1 on fold)

$59^{1}/_{8}$"

The lengths of the binding fabric and the hem ruffle (for sizes 4, 5, 6, and 7, respectively):
- For the neckline: $19^{3}/_{4}$", $19^{3}/_{4}$", $21^{5}/_{8}$", $21^{5}/_{8}$"
- For the hemline: $15^{3}/_{4}$", $15^{3}/_{4}$", $17^{3}/_{4}$", $17^{3}/_{4}$"
- For the hem ruffle: $55^{1}/_{8}$", $55^{1}/_{8}$", 57, $59^{1}/_{8}$"

Figure 4

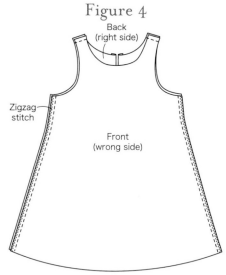

Back (right side)

Zigzag stitch

Front (wrong side)

Figure 5

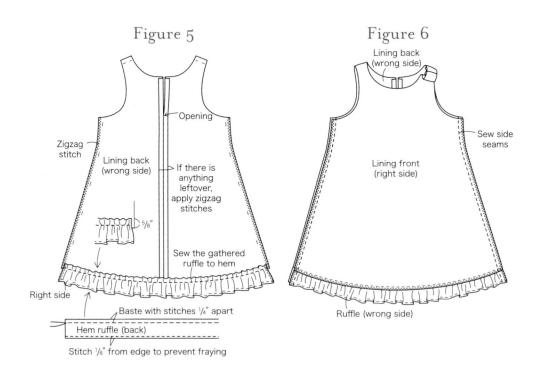

Opening

Zigzag stitch

Lining back (wrong side)

If there is anything leftover, apply zigzag stitches

5/8"

Sew the gathered ruffle to hem

Right side

Baste with stitches 1/4" apart

Hem ruffle (back)

Stitch 1/8" from edge to prevent fraying

Figure 6

Lining back (wrong side)

Sew side seams

Lining front (right side)

Ruffle (wrong side)

Figure 7

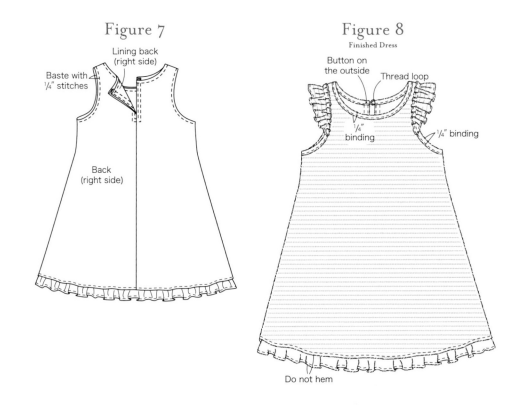

Lining back (right side)

Baste with 1/4" stitches

Back (right side)

Figure 8

Finished Dress

Button on the outside

Thread loop

1/4" binding

1/4" binding

Do not hem

Pants with Leg Warmers

Photograph on page 31.

Finished Measurements (for sizes 4, 5, 6, and 7, respectively)

Hips: 25¼", 26¾", 28⅜", 31½"
Length (waist to ankle): 28⅜", 30⅜", 32¼", 34¼"

Materials

* Pattern: 2-J from pattern insert (2 pattern pieces)
* Fabric: Fleece-lined cloth, as for sweatpants, 59⅛" wide. For sizes 4 and 5: 25⅝"; for sizes 6 and 7: 27½"
* Bulky weight tweed yarn: 50 grams
* U.S. size 10 knitting needles or a crochet hook
* Cord: ¼" × 43⅜"
* Lace thread, as needed

Gauge

14 stitches and 17 rows = 4" × 4" in stockinette stitch

Instructions

1. **Cut out the pattern pieces.** Following pattern 2-J in the back of the book, and referring to Figure 1, trace the patterns for the pants front and back onto a separate sheet of paper. Note the measurements of the patches; no patterns are necessary for these pieces.
2. **Cut the fabric.** Fold the fabric in half, selvage to selvage, right sides together. Position the pattern, and mark the patches as shown in Figure 2. Add a seam allowance to the fabric before cutting it.
3. **Make the buttonholes.** Using the but-

tonhole function on your machine, create the openings for the cord in the front of the pants, 1⅝" from the top edge. *See Figure 3.*
4. **Attach the front patch.** Hand stitch the two pieces for the front patch together to create one patch. Hand stitch to the pants front, as shown in Figure 3 or wherever you think it looks best.
5. **Make the right and left legs.** Place the left front on the left back, right sides together, and sew up the side seams and the inseam with a straight stitch. Go over each seam again using a zigzag stitch. Repeat for the right side. *See Figure 4.*
6. **Attach the left and right legs.** Place the left leg in the right leg, right sides together. Sew along the front, back, and crotch seam with a straight stitch. Go over the seam again using a zigzag stitch. Turn the pants right side out. *See Figure 5.*
7. **Attach the back patch.** Hand stitch the two pieces for the back patch together to create one patch. Hand stitch to the pants back, as shown in Figure 6 or wherever you think it looks best.
8. **Add the ties.** Fold the top of the waist under twice, and sew it in place around the pants. Pass the cord through the buttonholes.
9. **Knit the leg warmers.** Cast on 38 stitches for sizes 4 and 5 or 42 stitches for sizes 6 and 7 (alternately, crochet a chain 10¼" long for sizes 4 and 5 or a chain 11½" long for sizes 6 and 7). Work in a knit 2, purl 2 rib for 3" (approximately 13 rows). Switch to stockinette stitch, and work for 10¼" (approximately 45 rows). Cast off and finish the leg warmer by sewing the sides together.

10. **Attach the leg warmers.** Gather the hem of the pants as indicated. Place the wrong side of the leg warmer over the end of the right side of the leg. Hand stitch the leg warmer in place with lace thread. *See Figure 7.*

Figure 1

Pattern Details for 2-J

Pants back

Pants front

Front patch
4½"
4¾"
5"
5⅛"
3¼"
3½"
3¾"
4"

Back patch
4½"
4¾"
5"
5⅛"
2¼"
2⅜"
2⅝"
2¾"

The four measurements are for sizes 4, 5, 6, and 7, respectively

Figure 2

Pants Layout

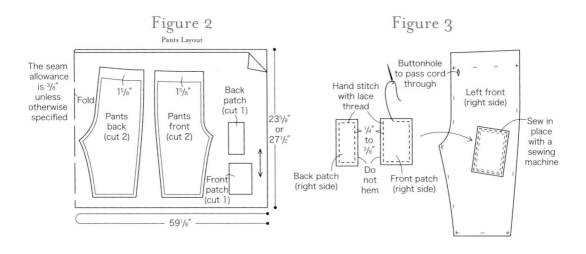

The seam allowance is ³/₈" unless otherwise specified

Fold

1⅝"

Pants back (cut 2)

1⅝"

Pants front (cut 2)

Back patch (cut 1)

Front patch (cut 1)

23⅝" or 27½"

59⅛"

Figure 3

Buttonhole to pass cord through

Hand stitch with lace thread

Back patch (right side)

Front patch (right side)

¼" to ³/₈"

Do not hem

Left front (right side)

Sew in place with a sewing machine

Figure 4

Back (right side)

Front (wrong side)

Side

Zigzag stitch both pieces together

Inseam

Zigzag stitch both pieces together

Figure 5

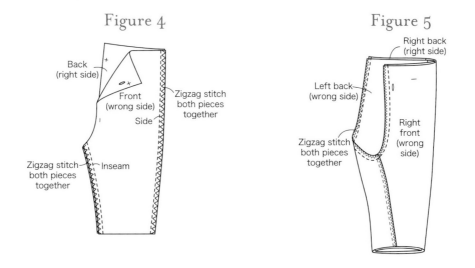

Right back (right side)

Left back (wrong side)

Right front (wrong side)

Zigzag stitch both pieces together

Figure 6

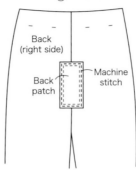

Back
(right side)

Back
patch

Machine
stitch

Figure 7

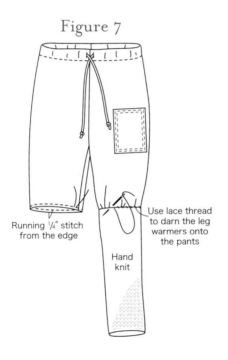

Running ¼" stitch
from the edge

Use lace thread
to darn the leg
warmers onto
the pants

Hand
knit

Figure 8

Finished Pants

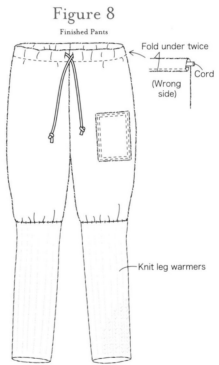

Fold under twice

Cord

(Wrong
side)

Knit leg warmers

Dress with Contrasting Patches

Photograph on page 35.

Finished Measurements (for sizes 4, 5, 6, and 7. respectively)

Chest: 26⅜", 28", 29½", 31¼"
Length: 26¾", 28⅜", 29½", 32¼"
Sleeve length: 14⅛", 15⅜", 17", 18½"

Materials

* Pattern: I-F from pattern insert (4 pattern pieces)
* Fabric: Cotton, 42½" wide. For sizes 4 and 5: 55⅛"; for sizes 6 and 7: 66⅞"
* Contrasting fabric scraps for appliqué squares, as needed
* Buttons: 7, ¼" to ⅝" in diameter
* Eye hook: I set
* Elastic tape: ¼" × 19¾"
* Thread for hand stitching, any 3 colors

Instructions

1. **Cut out the pattern pieces.** Following pattern I-F in the back of the book, and referring to Figure I, trace the patterns for the bodice back, bodice front, front facing, and sleeve onto a separate sheet of paper. Note the measurements of the skirt and the back facing; no patterns are necessary for these pieces.

2. **Cut the fabric.** Fold the fabric as shown in Figure 2. Position the pattern, and mark the skirt. Add a seam allowance to the fabric before cutting it. Cut the bias binding 45° to the fabric grain to the exact measurements shown.

3. **Make the front opening.** Sew the front facing, right side out, to the back of the bodice front using a zigzag stitch around the outer edge. Cut down the center of the bodice front and facing, and stitch around the opening. *See Figure 3.*

4. **Make the bodice back.** Fold the back facing in half lengthwise, right side out. Align the raw edges of the facing with the center edge of the right bodice back. Sew through all three layers along the edge, and then fold the facing over. Fold the center edge of the left bodice back toward the wrong side, and sew it in place. Place the left bodice back on the back facing, aligning the back centers. Pin the pieces in place and stitch across the facing along the bottom edge. *See Figure 4.*

5. **Attach the bodice front to the back.** Place the bodice front on the bodice back, right sides together. Sew across the shoulders and down the sides. Press the seams open. *See Figure 5.*

6. **Finish the neckline.** Attach the bias binding to the neckline, following the instructions on page 49.

7. **Sew the skirt.** Place the skirt front on the skirt back, right sides together, and sew along both sides. Fold the bottom hem under, and stitch it in place. Baste along the top edge of the skirt. Pull the ends of the thread to gather the fabric. *See Figure 5.*

8. **Sew the skirt to the bodice.** Place the skirt over the bodice, right sides together. Sew it in place using a zigzag stitch.

9. **Make the sleeves.** Fold the sleeve in half, right sides together, and sew along the underside of the sleeves, leaving room toward the cuff for the elastic to pass through. Fold the seam allowance under twice at the wrist end of the sleeve and stitch. Baste along the edge of the shoulder. *See Figure 6.*

10. **Attach the sleeves.** Pull the threads to gather the sleeves at the shoulders.

Place the sleeves in the bodice, right sides together, and stitch the sleeves in place. Finish by sewing the seam allowances together with a zigzag stitch. Pass the elastic through the openings at the wrist end of the sleeve. Hand stitch the openings closed.

11. **Attach the loops and buttons.** Make a thread loop following the instructions on page 68. Attach the loops to the back opening and sew the buttons on the opposite side. *See Figure 7.*

12. **Finish the dress.** Cut some of the fabric or contrasting fabric into squares and hand stitch them to the front of the dress. The size, position, and balance of the patches are up to you. *See Figure 8.*

Figure 1

Pattern Details for 1-F

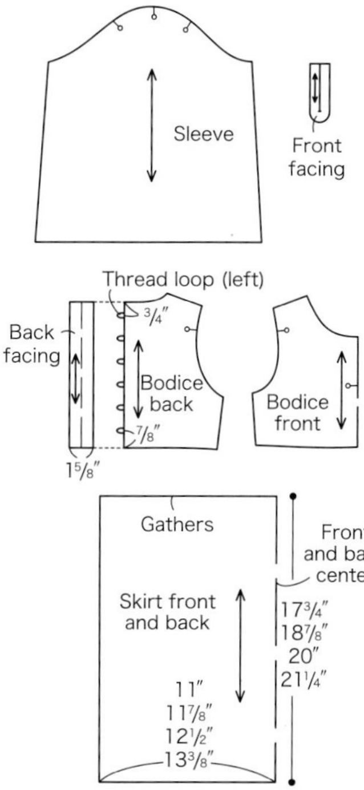

Sleeve

Front facing

Thread loop (left)

Back facing

Bodice back

3/4"

7/8"

1 5/8"

Bodice front

Gathers

Skirt front and back

Front and back center

17 3/4"
18 7/8"
20"
21 1/4"

11"
11 7/8"
12 1/2"
13 3/8"

The four measurements are for sizes 4, 5, 6, and 7, respectively

Figure 2

Dress Layout

Seam allowances are 3/8" unless otherwise specified

Back facing (cut 1)

Fold

Back (cut 2)

Front (cut 1 on fold)

Binding

1 1/2"

Front facing

55 1/8" or 66 7/8"

Sleeve (cut 1)

7/8"

Fold

Skirt front (cut 1 on fold)

3/4"

Sleeve (cut 1)

7/8"

Skirt back (cut 1)

3/4"

42 1/2" wide

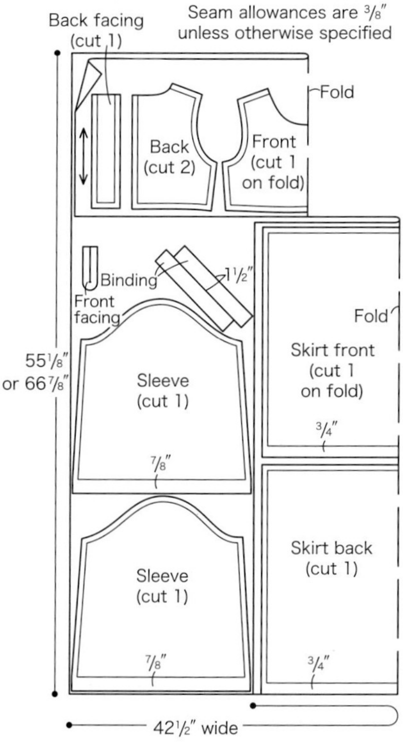

The length of the binding fabric (2 pieces) should be half the length of the neckline + 3/4".

Figure 3

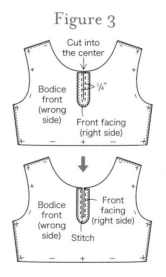

Cut into the center

Bodice front (wrong side)

1/4"

Front facing (right side)

Bodice front (wrong side)

Front facing (right side)

Stitch

Figure 4

Back facing

Zigzag stitch the three pieces together

Fold

Back facing (right side)

Right back (right side)

Back facing (right side)

Right back (right side)

Stitch

Fold the seam allowance under and stitch

Left back (right side)

Left back (right side)

Pin the center back together

Right back (right side)

Machine stitch the seam allowance

Figure 5

Machine stitch gathers, ¼″ basting stitch

Skirt (wrong side)

Figure 6

Sleeve (wrong side)

Machine stitch gathers

Sleeve (wrong side)

⁵⁄₈″ opening for elastic

opening for elastic

Fold under twice ⁵⁄₈″

³⁄₈″

Figure 7

Hook

Thread loop

Button

Thread loop

Figure 8

Button

Thread loop

Do not hem

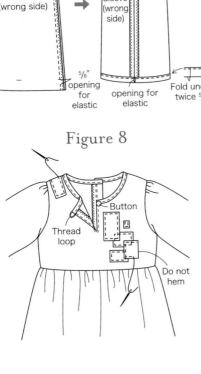

Figure 9

Finished View

¼″ binding

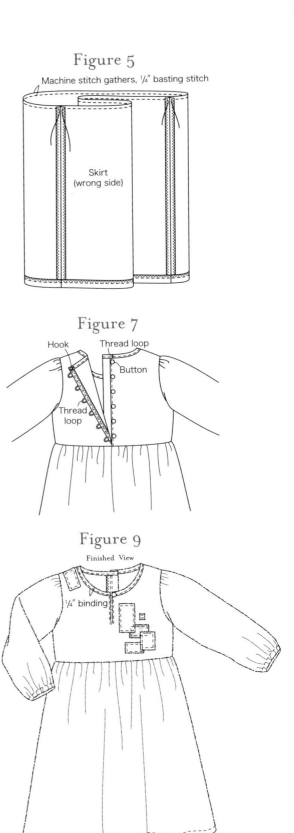

Lace-Trimmed Coat

Photograph on page 37.

Finished Measurements (for sizes 4, 5, 6, and 7, respectively)

Chest: 31¾", 33½", 35¼", 36⅝"
Length: 23¼", 25¼", 26⅞", 29¼"

Materials

* Pattern: 2-H from pattern insert (4 pattern pieces)
* Fabric: Linen, 43¼" wide. For sizes 4 and 5: 43¼"; for sizes 6 and 7: 51¼"
* Lining: Thin sheeting, 35¾" wide. For sizes 4 and 5: 51¼"; for sizes 6 and 7: 59⅛"
* Lace A: 1½" wide. For sizes 4 and 5: 51¼"; for sizes 6 and 7: 59⅛"
* Lace B: 1¼" wide. For sizes 4 and 5: 25⅝"; for sizes 6 and 7: 29½"
* Buttons: 8, ½" in diameter
* Snaps: 4 sets, ⅝" in diameter
* Eye hooks: 1 set
* Elastic: ¼" × 19¾"
* Lace thread, as needed

Instructions

1. **Cut out the pattern pieces.** Following pattern 2-H in the back of the book, and referring to Figure 1, trace the patterns for the coat sleeves and the longer patterns for the coat back and coat front onto a separate sheet of paper.

2. **Cut the fabric.** Fold the outer fabric in half, selvage to selvage, right sides together. Position the pattern as shown in Figure 2. Add a seam allowance to the fabric before cutting it. Fold the lining fabric in half, selvage to selvage, right sides together. Position the pattern as shown in Figure 3. Add a seam allowance before cutting it. Cut the bias binding 45° to the fabric grain to the exact measurements shown; no patterns are necessary for this piece.

3. **Attach the lace to the coat front.** Machine stitch lace A onto the opening edge of the front right and left sides, and then hand stitch it in place with lace thread. On the left front side, lay lace B on top of lace A and machine stitch it in place. *See Figure 4.*

4. **Sew the coat front to the back.** Place the two coat front pieces on the coat back, right sides together, and sew up the side seams. Press the seams open. Repeat for the lining.

5. **Make the sleeves.** Place the sleeve front on the sleeve back, right sides together, and stitch along both sides. Repeat for the lining. Fold the edge of the wrist under, toward the wrong side, and press. Repeat for the lining. Leave a gap for the elastic to pass through in the sleeve lining. *See Figure 5.*

6. **Attach the sleeves.** Place the sleeves in the bodices, right sides together, and sew along the raglan lines (see Figure 5 on page 94). Repeat for the lining. On the outer garment, press the seam allowance toward the sleeve. Hand stitch along the bodice side of the raglan seam with lace thread. Press the seam allowance of the lining toward the bodice.

7. **Attach the lining.** Place the coat bodice on the lining bodice, right sides together, and start sewing around the hem starting at the left front edge, moving across the bottom, up the right front edge. Turn the coat right

side out, and press. Stitch around the neckline close to the edge. *See Figure 6.*

8. **Finish the neckline.** Attach the bias binding to the neckline, following the instructions on page 49.

9. **Finish the sleeves.** Stitch the wrist openings of the outer fabric and lining together, and run elastic through them. *See Figure 7.*

10. **Finish the coat.** Make a thread loop following the instructions on page 68. Attach the loops to the coat opening, and sew the buttons on the opposite side. Hand stitch the snaps in place. *See Figure 7.*

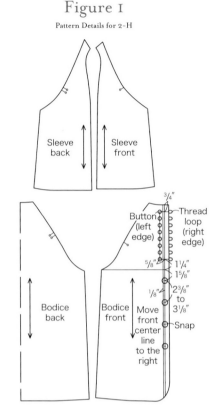

Figure 1

Pattern Details for 2-H

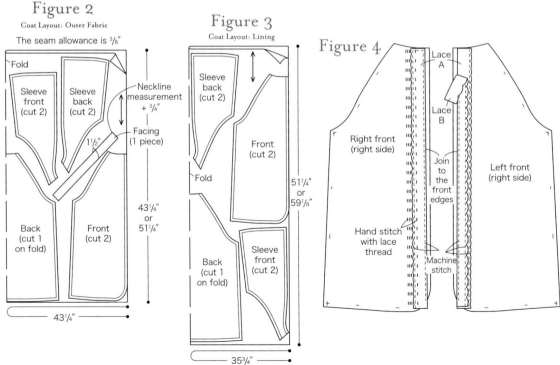

Figure 2

Coat Layout: Outer Fabric

The seam allowance is ³⁄₈″

Figure 3

Coat Layout: Lining

Figure 4

Figure 5

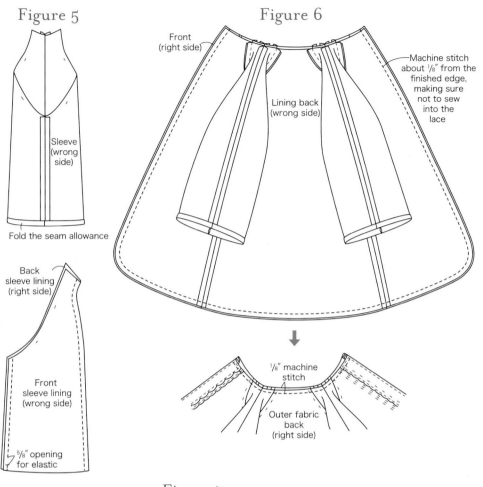

Sleeve
(wrong
side)

Fold the seam allowance

Back
sleeve lining
(right side)

Front
sleeve lining
(wrong side)

5/8" opening
for elastic

Figure 6

Front
(right side)

Lining back
(wrong side)

Machine stitch
about 1/8" from the
finished edge,
making sure
not to sew
into the
lace

1/8" machine
stitch

Outer fabric
back
(right side)

Figure 7

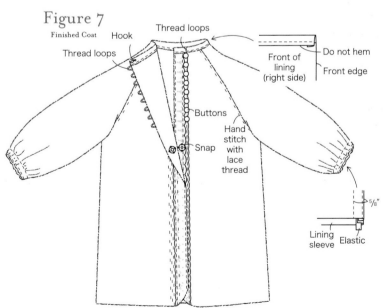

Finished Coat

Thread loops

Hook

Thread loops

Do not hem

Front of
lining
(right side)

Front edge

Buttons

Snap

Hand
stitch
with
lace
thread

5/8"

Lining
sleeve   Elastic

Scarf

Photograph on page 33.

Finished Measurements (one size)

42½" × 5⅛"

Materials

* Pattern: No pattern necessary
* Fabric remnants, as needed
* Lace scraps, as needed
* Lining: Wool, 43½" × 6"
* Buttons: 1, ⅞" in diameter; 9, ¾" in diameter
* Decorative bell: 1
* Thread for hand stitching: Gold, silver, and lace thread, as needed
* Leather cord: About 4"

Instructions

1. **Cut the fabric.** Cut the wool lining to 6" × 43½". *See Figure 1.*

2. **Sew the patchwork.** Sew the fabric remnants and lace together to form a piece of fabric a 6" × 43" with overlapping patterns. I have put together a set of remnants and lace that you can use as a standard, but don't worry about the measurements. Just sew together any fabrics that you like, and then hand stitch them as needed. *See Figure 2.*

3. **Attach the patchwork to the lining.** Place the patchwork strip on the lining, right sides together. Sew around three sides of the scarf, leaving a ⅜" seam allowance. *See Figure 3.*

4. **Finish the scarf.** Turn the scarf right side out, and press it with an iron. Fold the lining under ⅜" at the lace end, and sew. Attach a ruffle at the opposite end. Attach a decorative bell, buttons, and thread loop that can hook around a button. *See Figure 4.*

Figure 1

43¼"

6"   Wool

Figure 2

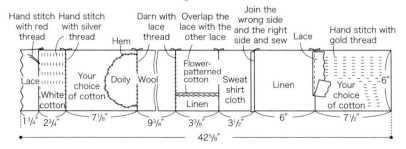

Hand stitch with red thread Hand stitch with silver thread Hem Darn with lace thread Overlap the lace with the other lace Join the wrong side and the right side and sew Lace Hand stitch with gold thread

Lace White cotton Your choice of cotton Doily Wool Flower-patterned cotton Linen Sweat shirt cloth Linen Your choice of cotton 6"

1¾" 2¾" 7⅛" 9¾" 3⅜" 3½" 6" 7½"

42⅝"

Figure 3

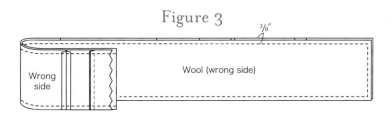

3/8"

Wrong side

Wool (wrong side)

Figure 4

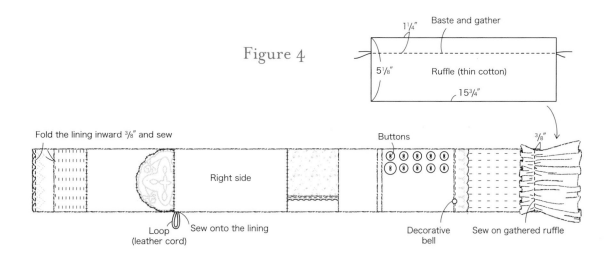

Baste and gather

1¼"

5⅛"

Ruffle (thin cotton)

15¾"

Fold the lining inward ⅜" and sew

Buttons

3/8"

Right side

Loop
(leather cord)

Sew onto the lining

Decorative
bell

Sew on gathered ruffle

White Melton Hat

Photograph on page 30.

Finished Measurements (S, M, and L, respectively)

Head circumference: 20½", 21¼", 22"

Materials

* Pattern: 2-K from pattern insert (2 pattern pieces)
* Fabric: Wool, 19¾" × 13¾"
* Contrasting fabric: Wool, 1¼" × 11⅞"
* Lining: Thin sheeting, 19¾" × 13¾"
* Button: 1, ⅞" in diameter
* Pom-pom: 1, 1⅝" in diameter
* Lace thread: Black, as needed

Instructions

1. **Cut out the pattern pieces.** Following pattern 2-K in the back of the book, and referring to Figure 1, trace the patterns for the top crown and side crown onto a separate sheet of paper.
2. **Cut the fabric.** Lay the outer fabric and lining flat. Position the pattern as shown in Figure 2. Add a seam allowance to the fabric before cutting it.
3. **Sew the outer hat.** Place an outer side crown on the outer top crown, right sides together, and sew them in place. Press the seams open. Repeat on the other side. *See Figure 3.*
4. **Add decorative stitches.** Hand stitch along the seams on the side crown with black lace thread. *See Figure 5.*
5. **Sew the lining.** Sew the lining together as you did for the outer hat. Press the seams open.
6. **Attach the lining.** Place the lining in the hat, right sides together. Place a tie cut out of contrasting fabric between the layers on one side and sew around the hat, leaving an opening along the back. *See Figure 6.*
7. **Shape the hat.** Turn the hat right side out, shape it, and hand stitch the opening shut. *See Figure 7.*
8. **Finish the hat.** Using your machine, make a buttonhole at the end of the tie. Attach a button on the opposite side. Attach the pom-pom to the top. *See Figure 8.*

Figure 1

Pattern Details for 2-K

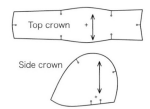

Figure 2

Hat Layout: Outer Fabric and Lining

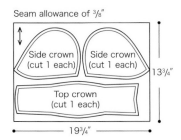

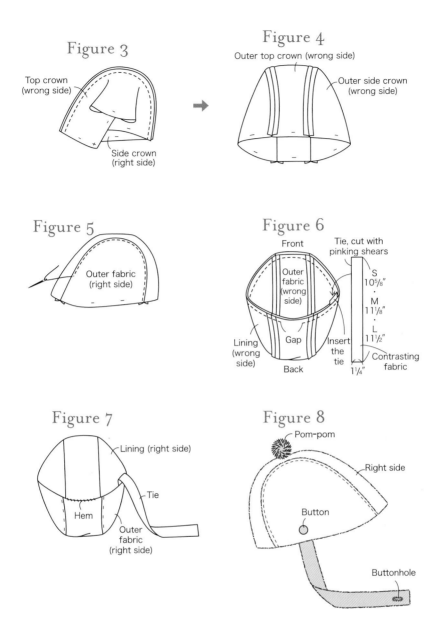

Figure 3

Top crown
(wrong side)

Side crown
(right side)

Figure 4

Outer top crown (wrong side)

Outer side crown
(wrong side)

Figure 5

Outer fabric
(right side)

Figure 6

Front

Tie, cut with
pinking shears

Outer
fabric
(wrong
side)

Lining
(wrong
side)

Gap

Insert
the
tie

Back

S
$10^{5}/_{8}$"
·
M
$11^{1}/_{8}$"
·
L
$11^{1}/_{2}$"

Contrasting
fabric

$1^{1}/_{4}$"

Figure 7

Lining (right side)

Tie

Hem

Outer
fabric
(right side)

Figure 8

Pom-pom

Right side

Button

Buttonhole

Coat with Scarf

Photograph on page 39.

Finished Measurements (for sizes 4, 5, 6, and 7, respectively)

Chest: 31½", 33", 34⅝", 36¼"
Length: 17¾", 19⅜", 20⅞", 22½"

Materials

* Pattern: 2-H from pattern insert (4 pattern pieces)
* Fabric: Melton cloth, 59⅛" wide. For sizes 4 and 5: 35½"; for sizes 43½"
* DK weight cotton yarn: 50 grams
* U.S. size 5 knitting needles
* Snaps: 3 sets, ¾" in diameter
* Eye hooks: 6 sets
* Buttons: 2, ¾" in diameter

Gauge

22 stitches and 22 rows = 4" × 4" in stockinette stitch

Note

In this garment, the left side folds over the right. If you would like the garment to fold over to the right side, put the hooks and concave snaps on the wrong side of the right front, and the eyes and convex snaps on the left front outer surface.

Instructions

1. **Cut out the pattern pieces.** Following pattern 2-H in the back of the book, and referring to Figure 1, trace the patterns for the sleeve and the shorter version of the patterns for the coat back and coat front onto a separate sheet of paper.

2. **Cut the fabric.** Fold the fabric in half, selvage to selvage, right sides together. Position the pattern as shown in Figure 2. Add a seam allowance before cutting it. Mark the positions of the decorative belt, the hooks, and the snaps based on the measurements shown. Cut the bias binding 45° to the fabric grain to the exact measurements shown. Cut the belt to the measurements shown. Patterns for the bias binding and the belt are not necessary.

3. **Hem the coat opening.** Fold the opening edge of the two coat front pieces under, toward the wrong side, and stitch it in place ⅝" from the edge.

4. **Attach the coat front to the back.** Place the two coat front pieces on the coat back, right sides together. Sew up the side seams, and press the seams open. Fold under the bottom hem, and sew it in place 1⅝" from the bottom edge.

5. **Make the sleeves.** Lay the sleeve front on the sleeve back, right sides together, and sew the underside seams and shoulder seams. Press the seams open. Fold under the wrist hem, and stitch in place. *See Figure 3.*

6. **Attach the sleeves.** Place the sleeves in the bodice, right sides together, and sew along the raglan lines. Turn the coat right side out. *See Figure 4.*

7. **Finish the neckline.** Attach the bias binding to the neckline, following the instructions on page 49. *See Figure 5.*

8. **Make the decorative belt.** Place the two pieces of fabric for the decorative belt wrong sides together. Stitch around all four sides. Attach the belt to the back of the coat with buttons. *See Figure 6.*

9. **Attach the snaps and hooks.** Referring to the diagram for placement, sew the

eye hooks and snaps to the front edge of the coat. *See Figure 7.*

10. **Knit the scarf.** Cast on 22 stitches. Purl 1, then knit to the end of the row. Continue in this manner, purling the first stitch of each row, until the scarf is 27½" (approximately 154 rows) for size 4 and 5 and 28⅜" (approximately 158 rows) for sizes 6 and 7. Cast off.

11. **Finish the coat.** Hand stitch the scarf to the back neckline. *See Figure 8.*

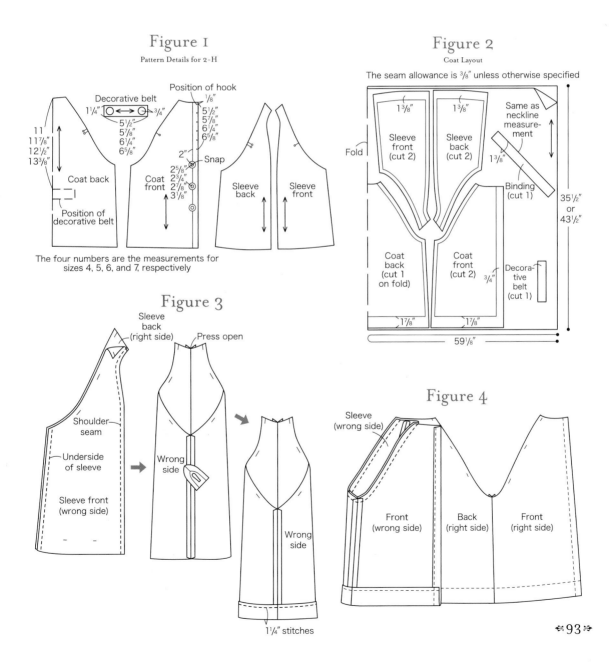

Figure 1

Pattern Details for 2-H

The four numbers are the measurements for sizes 4, 5, 6, and 7, respectively

Figure 2

Coat Layout

The seam allowance is ⅜" unless otherwise specified

Figure 3

Figure 4

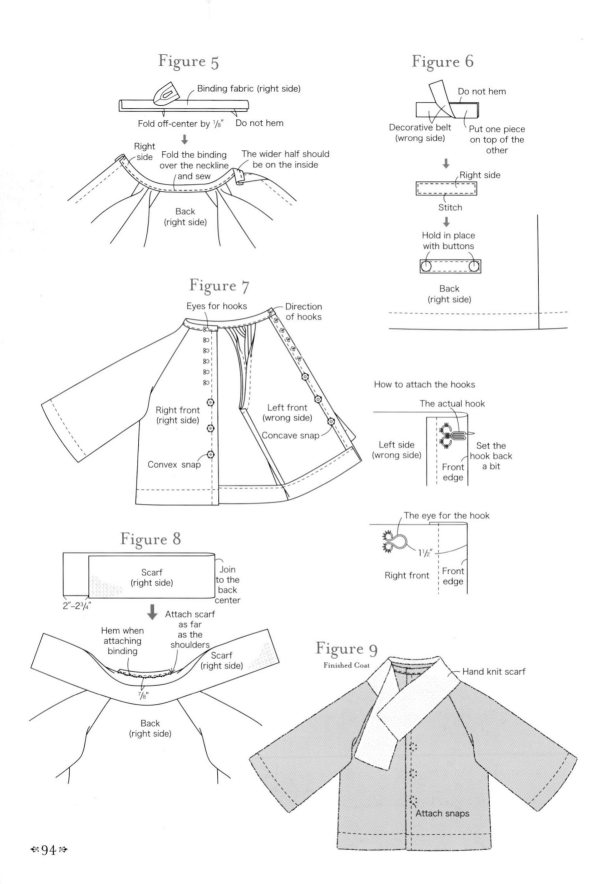

Figure 5

Binding fabric (right side)

Fold off-center by 1/8"   Do not hem

↓

Right side   Fold the binding over the neckline and sew   The wider half should be on the inside

Back (right side)

Figure 6

Do not hem

Decorative belt (wrong side)   Put one piece on top of the other

↓

Right side

Stitch

↓

Hold in place with buttons

Back (right side)

Figure 7

Eyes for hooks   Direction of hooks

Right front (right side)

Left front (wrong side)

Concave snap

Convex snap

How to attach the hooks

The actual hook

Left side (wrong side)   Set the hook back a bit

Front edge

The eye for the hook

1 1/2"

Right front   Front edge

Figure 8

Scarf (right side)   Join to the back center

2"–2 3/4"

↓

Hem when attaching binding   Attach scarf as far as the shoulders   Scarf (right side)

7/8"

Back (right side)

Figure 9

Finished Coat   Hand knit scarf

Attach snaps

Pants

Photograph on page 30.

Finished Measurements (for sizes 4, 5, 6, and 7, respectively)

Hips: 29⅛", 30¾", 32¼", 33¾"
Length (waist to ankle): 17", 18¾", 20½", 22⅛"

Materials

* Pattern: 2-I from pattern insert (1 pattern piece)
* Fabric: Cotton, 35½" wide. For sizes 4 and 5: 43¼"; for sizes 6 and 7: 51¼"
* Lace: ⅞" wide. For sizes 4 and 5: 35½"; for sizes 6 and 7: 39⅜"
* Elastic: ¼" wide and slightly shorter than the waist measurement

Instructions

1. **Cut out the pattern pieces.** Following pattern 2-I in the back of the book, and referring to Figure I, trace the patterns for the pants onto a separate sheet of paper.

2. **Cut the fabric.** Fold the fabric in half, selvage to selvage, right sides together. Position the pattern as shown in Figure 2. Add a seam allowance to the fabric before cutting it.

3. **Make the legs.** Fold the pants left in half, right sides together, and sew up the inseam. Finish the seam using zig-zag stitches. Repeat for the pants right.

4. **Attach the lace.** Place lace along the inside of the pant legs at the bottom edge, so that about ⅜" of lace shows. Sew it in place. *See Figure 3.*

5. **Attach the legs.** Place the left leg inside the right leg, right sides together, and sew along the front, back, and crotch seam. Leave some space in the back waistband to pass elastic through. Finish the seam using zigzag stitches, but leave a notch open where you are going to insert the elastic.

6. **Finish the pants.** Fold the edge of the waist under, toward the wrong side, twice. Sew it in place, leaving a small opening for the elastic. Run the elastic through, and hand stitch the opening closed. *See Figure 3.*

Figure I

Pattern Details for 2-I

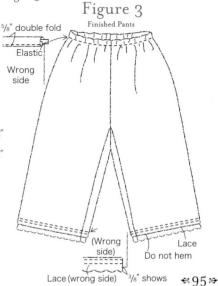

Pants
left and right

Make it ¾" longer

Figure 2 Layout

The seam allowance is ⅜" unless otherwise specified

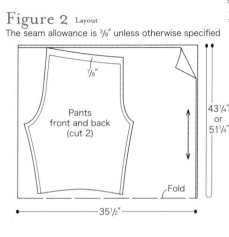

⅞"

Pants
front and back
(cut 2)

Fold

43¼"
or
51¼"

35½"

Figure 3

⅝" double fold   Finished Pants

Elastic

Wrong
side

(Wrong
side)

Lace
Do not hem

Lace (wrong side)   ⅜" shows

☙❧☙ ☙❧☙ ☙❧☙ ☙❧☙

JUNKO OKAWA is both a hairstylist and a designer. She chose the name Łąka
for this collection of distinctive and comfortable girls' clothing. For each
project, she selected the materials, drew the
patterns, and made the finished garments.

TRUMPETER BOOKS
An imprint of Shambhala Publications, Inc.
Horticultural Hall
300 Massachusetts Avenue
Boston, Massachusetts 02115
www.shambhala.com

9 8 7 6 5 4 3 2 1

First English Edition
Printed in China

♾ This edition is printed on acid-free paper that meets the American
National Standards Institute z39.48 Standard.
♻ Shambhala Publications makes every effort to print on recycled paper.
For more information please visit www.shambhala.com.

Distributed in the United States by Random House, Inc.,
and in Canada by Random House of Canada Ltd

Designed by Daniel Urban-Brown

Library of Congress Cataloging-in-Publication Data
Okawa, Junko.
Carefree clothes for girls: 20 patterns for outdoor frocks, playdate dresses, and more/
Junko Okawa.—1st ed.
p. cm.
ISBN 978-1-59030-717-5 (pbk.: alk. paper)
1. Girls' clothing—Juvenile literature. 2. Dressmaking—Patterns—Juvenile literature.
I. Title.
TT562.O383 2009
646.4'06—dc22
2009010254

☙❧☙ ☙❧☙ ☙❧☙ ☙❧☙